A Timeline
of Boston

A Timeline of Boston

A Chronological History

by Jim Vrabel

COMMONWEALTH EDITIONS
AN IMPRINT OF APPLEWOOD BOOKS
CARLISLE, MASSACHUSETTS

ISBN 978-1-933212-12-8

Published by Commonwealth Editions
an imprint of Applewood Books
Carlisle, Massachusetts 01741
www.commonwealtheditions.com

Commonwealth Editions publishes books about the history, traditions, and beauty of places in New England and throughout America for adults and children.

To request a free copy of our current print catalog featuring our best-selling books, write to:
Applewood Books
P.O. Box 27
Carlisle, MA 01741

Book design by Nakeesha Barron

MANUFACTURED IN THE UNITED STATES OF AMERICA

Contents

ILLUSTRATIONS

LEGEND

The entries contained in *A Timeline of Boston* are arranged in chronological order as nearly as possible. Each entry is marked by an icon denoting various topic categories. The icons and the list of categories are as follows:

	Population/Immigration
	Planning/Development
	Buildings: Public/Commercial/Residential
	Transportation/Water/Municipal Services
	Parks/Public Art/Cemeteries
	Settlement/War/Boston History
	Politics
	Social Change
	Society/Hotels/Restaurants/Visitors
	Crime/Public Safety/Law
	Disasters/Tragedies
	Nature
	Religion
	Education
	Health/Science/Technology
	Business/Labor
	Media
	The Arts: Visual Art/Letters & Literature/Music/Theater/Popular Culture
	Sports/Recreation

Note and Legend:
An asterisk early in an entry indicates it is an "Old Style" date (prior to the adoption of the Gregorian calendar in 1752). An asterisk at the end of an entry indicates that a related entry appears in that later year. Events that took place between January 1 and March 24 prior to 1752 (when March 25 marked the beginning of the English calendar year) have been moved into the next year.

FOREWORD TO THE ORIGINAL EDITION
OF *WHEN IN BOSTON*

As any enthusiast captivated with the history of Boston soon learns, there is good news and there is bad news. The good news is that Boston's age is so great (nearly four hundred years) and its history so colorful that it never ceases to provide topics for historians to explore and narratives for readers to enjoy. Politics and religion, war and peace, education and medicine, science and economics, fine arts and architecture, philosophy and literature, immigration and transportation, sports and recreation—these and many other topics can be found in the extraordinary number of books and articles about Boston.

The bad news is that the amount of material relating to Boston history is so enormous, and the number of publications so extensive, that it is almost impossible for readers and researchers to recall the location of certain references, remember the date of particular events, or come up with the correct titles of specific prominent figures. Where did I see that reference? What year was that election held? When did they launch that ship? When was so-and-so mayor? When did that battle take place? What book contained that particular quotation? Where can I find what the city's population was just before the Civil War? These are the kinds of questions that haunt writers when they are trying to go back and verify a fact, locate a date, or find the original source of a statement. It was all very frustrating until Jim Vrabel came along.

I first met Jim Vrabel over a cup of coffee when we were talking about his recent experiences as coauthor of a biographical study of Pope John Paul II. From there we wandered off into a broader discussion of Boston history and local politics, and I was greatly impressed with the range of Jim's knowledge about the city of Boston. Some of his information, I learned, came from his own long-standing fascination with the city's history; some of it came from his firsthand experiences working in city government as assistant director of the Mayor's Office of Neighborhood Services, executive assistant to the Boston School Committee, and, finally, in his current position as senior research analyst and editor at the Boston Redevelopment Authority.

Toward the end of our conversation, I asked Jim if he was involved in any other projects now that the book about Pope John Paul II had been published. Almost as an afterthought, he reached into his briefcase and pulled out a sizable manuscript that was obviously still in progress and handed it to me. As soon as I looked at it, lights flashed and whistles blew. It was great! I wanted a copy for myself. Jim had developed an impressive compendium of facts, figures, and events in Boston, arranged as a continuous time line. Starting with the early voyages of discovery, the native people who occupied these shores, and the arrival of John Winthrop and the Puritans, the subjects move chronologically through the colonial period to the struggle for independence and the formation of the Constitution that made Boston part of the new nation. From the social and industrial changes of the early nineteenth century to the fight for women's rights and the crusade against slavery, *When in Boston* offers the reader events and personalities of the Civil War period and the postwar years, when immigration changed the face of the city. In addition to ethnic diversity, Vrabel describes the libraries, museums, theaters, and music halls that went up in the city at a time when professional sports teams were just making their appearance. Modern Boston politics, the creation of a New Boston, the rise of racial conflict, the busing crisis, and the new waves of immigrants are among the innumerable topics that will either refresh readers' memories or provide them with all sorts of new information.

Jim Vrabel not only compiles this impressive list of subjects, topics, people, buildings, places, activities, and events associated with Boston history, all arranged in chronological order, but also further divides the material into categories that include Population/Immigration, Planning/Development, Politics, Social Change, Religion, Education, the Arts, and even Sports/Recreation, making it possible for readers to go back and extract the specific information they are interested in. There is no doubt that *When in Boston* will prove to be an invaluable research tool for academics, scholars, researchers, graduate students, librarians, archivists, museum directors, newspaper editors, and all those whose professional lives and careers are centered on the study of Boston. But this handy, single-volume reference work will also be a very welcome addition to the bookshelves and libraries of all those general readers who love the city and its history. Vrabel has succeeded in his task, not only because of his extensive personal knowledge about Boston history, but also because of his innate love of order and his keen sense of what's important to remember about the city's past.

THOMAS H. O'CONNOR
Boston College
2004

NOTE:
A Timeline of Boston is a shorter version of When In Boston: A Timeline & Almanac, originally published in 2004 and recently reissued by Applewood Books. Anyone wishing to obtain a copy of that more comprehensive 400-page timeline of Boston history can do so through the Applewood website (awb.com) or through the websites of the large Internet booksellers. Those with comments or questions on either book may contact the author at jimvrabel@gmail.com.

Acknowledgments

Most of all, I want to thank the late Thomas O'Connor of Boston College, Boston's foremost modern historian, for helping to make this book and its predecessor a reality. I want to thank historians William Fowler of Northeastern University and Robert Allison of Suffolk University for their support and encouragement. I also want to thank all of the archivists and librarians for their assistance, including Peter Drummey of the Massachusetts Historical Society; Nancy Richard, formerly of the Bostonian Society; Marta Pardee-King, Mary Devine, Linda MacIver, Henry Scannell, Aaron Schmidt, and Gayle Fithian of the Boston Public Library; John Cronin, formerly of the *Boston Herald*, and Lisa Tuite of the *Boston Globe*; John McColgan and Dave Nathan of the Boston City Archives; Mary Warnement of the Boston Athenaeum; Robert Fleming of Emerson College; Bridget Carr of the Boston Symphony Orchestra; Donna Wells of the Boston Police Department, and the late George Sanborn of the state Transportation Library.

For their contributions of information and friendship, I want to thank Bob Consalvo, Greg Perkins, and John Avault, formerly or currently of the Boston Redevelopment Authority; and Richard Tourangeau, Marilyn Miller, Larry Rothstein, Lew Finfer, and Sue Goganian.

Finally, I would like to thank all of the people formerly at Northeastern University Press, which did so much to carry the torch to preserve and promote Boston history, and Phil Zuckerman, Barbara DaSilva and all of the people currently at Applewood Books, which has picked up that torch and is continuing that effort.

Preface

Historians have a difficult job. They must reconstruct a *whole past* from the *pieces* available in the present. They are also expected to tell history as a *story*. In *A Timeline of Boston*, I have tried to select the most significant *pieces* of Boston history and present them in the order in which they occurred to suggest the many *stories* that make up the city's history.

The entries in this book can be read straight through as a shorthand history of Boston. Or, readers can pick and choose, following the subjects that interest them. The index can be used to turn this into a reference book and the street index into a visitors' guide.

A Timeline of Boston is meant to be used as much as read. It offers the "greatest hits" of the *who*, *what*, and *where* as well as the *when* of Boston history. But it is also meant to whet the appetite and encourage readers to explore the many other books on Boston history that explain the *how* and *why*.

Boston Latin graduate George Santayana famously warned that "those who cannot remember the past are condemned to repeat it." But he also advised that "the more you know, the more beautiful everything is." I hope that this book can help the city and its history to become more beautiful and more meaningful by reminding people what happened—and when—in Boston.

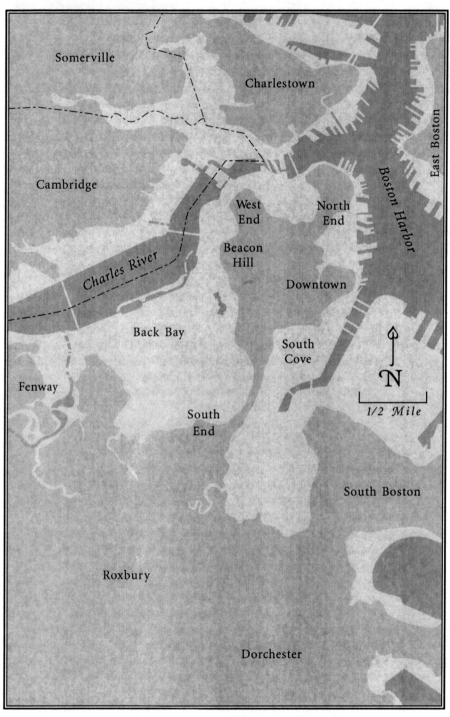

Somerville

Charlestown

East Boston

Cambridge

West End

North End

Boston Harbor

Beacon Hill

Charles River

Downtown

Back Bay

South Cove

N

Fenway

1/2 Mile

South End

South Boston

Roxbury

Dorchester

Map of Boston and environs showing the original land areas (medium gray) and areas built on landfill (pale gray).
(Map by Charles Bahne)

1000 – 1699

1000 (ca.)

According to Norse legend, **Leif Ericson** arrives in North America. Although no physical evidence exists today, his description of arriving at a place where a river (today's Charles?) runs through a lake (the Back Bay?) into the sea (Boston Harbor?) prompts some to speculate that he may have reached present-day Boston. A statue of Leif Ericson by **Anne Whitney** is erected on the **Commonwealth Avenue Mall** near Kenmore Square in 1887.

1600

By this time, Eastern Algonquin Indians have come to inhabit the area in which today's Boston lies. The local tribes include the *Massachusetts*, *Nipmucks*, *Pocumtucks*, and *Pokanokets* (or *Wampanoags*).

1614

Captain John Smith explores Boston Harbor. In his *A Description of New England*, he mentions a river the Indians called the *Quineboquin*. Later, he tells the young Prince Charles to change the names on his map to some "good English ones" and the prince proceeds to name the **Charles River** after himself.

1615

A series of epidemics from diseases brought by the European explorers and settlers (chicken pox, measles, scarlet fever, smallpox, etc.) begins and over the next few years kills as many as 90% of the estimated 75,000 Indians who had been living in New England.

1621

September 18.* **Miles Standish** and a party from the Plymouth Colony (est. 1620) explore **Boston Harbor**. Standish later reports: "Better harbors for shipping cannot be, than there are. At the entrance of the bay are many rocks and islands, and in all likelihood, very good fishing ground. Many, yea, most of the islands have been inhabited, some being cleared from end to end, but the people are all dead or removed."

1623

September. After an unsuccessful attempt the year before, Robert Gorges leads a party that settles at *Wessagussett* (today's Weymouth). Among the settlers are **Samuel Maverick**, who later establishes a trading post at *Winnisimmett* (later Chelsea); **Thomas Walford**, who later leads a party that settles at *Mishawum* (later Charlestown); and **Rev. William Blackstone** (or Blaxton).

1625 (ca.)

Rev. William Blackstone, a 27-year-old Anglican clergyman described by Walter Muir Whitehill as "a bachelor with a taste for his own company," settles on the 487-acre

Trimount in 1630, decoration from Engine 15, *by Samuel Lancaster Gerry and James Burt, oil on panel, 1836.* (Courtesy of the Bostonian Society)

peninsula which the Indians call *Mushauwomuk.* (English settlers later shorten the name to *Shawmut,* then call it Trimount, Tramount, or Trimountaine, for the three peaks on today's Beacon Hill.) The first European settler of today's Boston, Blackstone builds a cabin near the corner of today's **Spruce** and **Beacon Streets** on **Beacon Hill**.

1629

 March 4.* **Charles I** grants a charter to the **Massachusetts Bay Company** for land that extends from three miles north of the Merrimack River to three miles south of the Charles River. By this time, the company is made up of a group of Puritans, who had bought up controlling shares from the original members. Later in the year, the members of the Massachusetts Bay Company sign the Agreement at Cambridge, which states that "the whole government, together with the patent of the said plantation . . . remain with us and others who shall inhabit upon the said plantation." Meeting in a "General Court," the company elects John Winthrop governor, John Humphrey deputy governor, and 18 others as "assistants."

1630

 March 22. The *Arbella* sets sail from Southampton, England. It is one of 11 ships carrying approximately 700 members of the Massachusetts Bay Company that departs in the next few months. En route, **John Winthrop** writes (and probably delivers) an address entitled "A Modell of Christian Charity," in which he declares: "For wee must Consider that wee shall be as a Citty upon a Hill. The eies of all people are upon Us." The *Arbella* and four other ships land at Salem on July 12*, but the members of the Massachusetts Bay Company do not find the settlement to their liking and relocate to **Charlestown**. Other ships also arrive from England and, by the end of the summer, the population of this settlement reaches an estimated 1,500 people, most of them living in tents and lean-tos.

July 30. The **First Church in Boston** is established, initially in Charlestown. It is the third church in the English settlements. The congregation initially worships under a large tree, "the Charlestown Oak," then moves to a mud-walled, thatched-roof church at today's **27 State Street** in September 1632. The congregation becomes Unitarian in the 1780s and moves to its current location at **66 Marlborough Street** in the Back Bay in 1868.

August. **William Blackstone** informs the Charlestown settlers of the presence of fresh water springs on the Shawmut Peninsula. He invites **Isaac Johnson**, whom he had known in England, to share his cabin. **John Winthrop** and a group of approximately 150 additional members of the Massachusetts Bay Company follow, living in huts and wigwams.

*September 7.** Meeting as a Court of Assistants in Charlestown, the leaders of the Massachusetts Bay Company vote: "that Trimountaine shalbe called **Boston**," after the town in Lincolnshire from which many of the Puritans had come. On October 19, meeting as a General Court, the company decides to transfer the government from Charlestown to Boston. Winthrop later writes that the company "had all things to doe, as in the beginning of the world."

1631

March. Massachusetts sachem **Chickataubut** visits Boston "with his sannops and squaws." A dinner is held in the chief's honor, where, according to Winthrop, he "behaved himself as soberly as an Englishman." Chickataubut returns in April, seeking to trade for a new suit. Winthrop, however orders his tailor to put the chief "into a very good new suit from head to foot," at the governor's own expense.

Spring. Deputy Governor **Thomas Dudley** moves to the newly established settlement of Newtowne (later **Cambridge**). Governor **John Winthrop** begins to build a house there as well but is subsequently persuaded to remain in Boston. He has the unfinished house dismantled and reassembled near Town Cove. On May 18, in the first election to be held in Boston, Winthrop is re-elected governor "by the general consent of the Whole Court, manifested by the erection of hands. . ."

1632

Boston's population is estimated at slightly more than 200.

Boston Neck, which was at the intersection of today's **Washington** and **Berkeley Streets** in the South End, is fortified to protect the town from Indian attacks. It is an isthmus 40 yards wide which is sometimes flooded over at high tide. Some type of barrier or guard post is maintained there until 1832.

Summer. The **First Church in Roxbury** opens at today's **John Eliot Square**. John Eliot is named the first "teacher," and he preaches here for more than 60 years. The current church, designed by William Blaney and containing a 1,500-pound bell cast by Paul Revere and a clock built by Simon Willard, is dedicated on June 7, 1804.

October 3. The General Court of the Massachusetts Bay Company is permanently established in Boston, which is declared "the fittest place for publique meetings of any place in the Bay."

Smoking is banned in public. A law is passed which prohibits the use of "tobacco in any inne, or common victual house, except in a private room there, so as the master of said house nor any guest there shall take offence." The fine for breaking the law is two shillings and sixpence for every offense.

1633

March 4. **Robert Coles** of Roxbury is found guilty of drunkenness and ordered to "weare about his neck & soe hange upon his outward garment a D made of redd clothe & sett upon white; to contynue for a yeare and not to leave it off at any tyme when he comes amongt company under penalty of XLs."

The General Court rules "that the Indians had a just right to such lands as they possessed and improved by subduing the same."

October 8. The first town meeting in the Colonies is held in the Dorchester Meeting House at the intersection of today's **East Cottage** and **Pleasant Streets**. The purpose of the meeting is "to sette down such orders as may tend to the generall good."

1634

March 4.* **Samuel Cole** opens the first tavern in Boston at today's **239 Washington Street**. Its prices for both food and drink are set by the General Court.

May 14. The "Winthrop Mutiny" takes place at a meeting of the General Court in the First Church Meeting House at today's **27 State Street**. Citizens, upset to learn that, under the charter, elections were supposed to have been held annually—but were not—turn Winthrop out of office and elect Thomas Dudley governor.

July. The first fort is built on **Castle Island** in today's South Boston. A mud-walled structure, it is replaced a number of times. Construction of the current **Fort Independence** began in 1834 and was completed in 1851.

August. **Boston Common** is established. The first public open space in the Colonies, it is acquired when the town purchases 44 of the 50 acres of land that it had allowed William Blackstone to retain. Later records describe how "the Town laid out a place for a trayning field; which is used for that purpose & for the feeding of Cattell." When some advocate selling the land for development in 1640, the town orders: "Henceforth there shalbe noe land granted for hous-plott or garden out of Comon Field."

October. **William Blackstone** leaves Boston, complaining, "I left England on account of the Bishops. I fear that I may have to leave here on account of the Brethren." He eventually settles in what is today Rhode Island.

Portrait of John Winthrop,
second governor of Massachusetts.
Engraving by O'Pelton.
(Courtesy of the Bostonian Society)

1635

The town enacts its first zoning ordinance. The order reads: "There shall noe house at all be built in this towne neere unto any of the streets and laynes therein but with the advise and consent of the overseers of the towne's occasions for the avoyding of disorderly building to the inconvenience of streets and laynes and for the more comely and Commodius ordering of them."

March 4*. It is voted to erect a beacon on Sentry Hill (thereafter **Beacon Hill**) "to give notice to the country of any danger." The beacon is constructed a year later, rebuilt in 1768, and torn down by British troops in 1775. It is later replaced several times. The current version, located off **Bowdoin Street** near the original site, was erected in 1898.

April 13. **Boston Latin School** is established when town meeting votes to entreat "Our Brother **Philomen Pormort** to become schole master for the teaching and nourtering of children with us." The oldest public school in America, its graduates would include Cotton Mather, Sam Adams, John Hancock, Charles Bulfinch, Ralph Waldo Emerson, Edward Everett Hale, George Santayana, and Leonard Bernstein (Benjamin Franklin attended the school briefly). Classes are held initially in Pormort's home, then in a new building at today's **45 School Street** in 1645. The school moves several times, arriving at its current location at **78 Avenue Louis Pasteur** in 1922.

The first town jail ("gaol") opens on Prison Lane, today's **Court Square**. Built of wood with barred windows, it is later described by Hawthorne in *The Scarlet Letter*. The jail is later moved to Leverett Street in 1822, then to today's **215 Charles Street** in 1851. Designed by Gridley J.F. Bryant, the granite building continues in use until 1991 and is converted to the Liberty Hotel in 2007.

1636

October 28. **Harvard College** is established when the General Court awards 400 pounds for construction of "a schoale or colledge... the next Court to appoint where and what building." A year later, the General Court directs that the school be located in Newtowne, and changes the community's name to Cambridge, after the university town in England. The college opens in 1638. It is named for the **Rev. John Harvard**, a 27-year-old minister who dies of consumption after living for only a year in Charlestown and leaves his 320-volume library and half his estate to the new college. Nathaniel Eaton is the first master. He is subsequently accused of beating students with a walnut cudgel and his wife is accused of mixing goat dung in the hasty pudding. The couple flees to Virginia at the end of the first school year, and the college closes temporarily before reopening in 1640.

1637

September 28. **William Schouler** and **John Williams** become the first men executed for murder in Boston, when they are hanged on **Boston Common**. Schouler is convicted of murdering a servant girl whose body was found in the woods by an Indian Williams of murdering a man with whom he had escaped from prison.

November 8. **Anne Hutchinson** is banished for heresy. A midwife and lay healer who lived at today's **238 Washington Street**, she is an Antinomian and believes that "grace" alone is necessary for salvation—rather than in combination with "good works." Although she had many supporters in the town, her critics include Winthrop, who confides in his journal: "if she had attended to her household affairs and such things as belong to women, and not gone out of her way and calling to meddle in such things as are proper for men, whose minds are stronger."

1638

February 26. The **Desire** arrives from Providence Island in the West Indies, with the first slaves to come to Boston aboard.

March 13. The **Ancient and Honorable Artillery Company** is chartered. Established the year before as the Military Company of Massachusetts, the organization assumes its current name in 1737. Its headquarters are later located first in the Town House, at the site of today's Old State House at **210 Washington Street**. It moves to the third floor of **Faneuil Hall** in 1746 and its headquarters are still located there today.

1639

May 20. The **Mather School** is founded. The first free, public school in America supported by taxes, it opens soon after on today's **Pleasant Street** in Dorchester with six boys in the first class. The school is supported by the fees paid by farmers who graze their cattle on Thompson Island. Girls are first admitted in 1748. The current school building, designed by Cram, Goodhue and Ferguson, opens on **Meeting House Hill** in 1905.

November 5. A post office is established in a tavern located near the corner of today's **Washington** and **Devonshire Streets**. The first in the Colonies, tavern proprietor

A view of Boston Common. (Courtesy of the Bostonian Society)

Richard Fairbanks is Boston's first postmaster. Designated as the place for "all letters from beyond the sea, or are to be sent thither," it handles only overseas mail. Those wishing to send or receive mail within the Colonies must make their own arrangements with private travelers.

Edward Palmer becomes the first man placed in the stocks in Boston. The builder of the device, he is punished for submitting a bill which is judged to be exorbitant. A few months later, a convicted bigamist is sentenced to be "set in the stocks for one hour on Lecture Day for two weeks so that all maids and widows might see him and not become number three."

1640
August 27. An explosion aboard the ***Mary Rose*** sinks the British man-of-war in Boston Harbor, killing 14 people. Shortly before the ammunition explosion, the captain had declined Gov. John Winthrop's invitation to bring his crew ashore for church services, declaring they would hold their own services on board the ship.

1641
The General Court passes the first law against cruelty to animals. The law states "that no man shall exercise any tyranny or cruelty towards any brute creatures which are usually kept for the use of man."

An African-American maidservant is welcomed into a Dorchester church, according to John Winthrop, because of her "sound knowledge and true godliness."

1642
March 27. It is voted that beer should be provided at town meetings.

August. The ***Trial*** is launched from Nehemiah Bourne's wharf in the North End. At 160 tons, it is the first full-size ship built in Boston and is later credited with initiating Boston's foreign trade.

1643

 January 18. On this day, according to Ebenezer Clapp's ***History of Dorchester***, "there were strange sights seen about Castle Island, and the Governor's Island. . . in form like a man, that would sometimes cast flames and sparkles of fire. This was seen about eight of the clock in the evening by many. About the same time a voice was heard between Boston and Dorchester upon the water in a dreadful manner, crying out, 'Boy, boy, come away, come away.'"

 May 10. The General Court divides the Massachusetts Bay Colony into four shires, or counties: **Suffolk** (which includes Boston and seven neighboring towns), **Norfolk**, **Essex**, and **Middlesex**.

 Anne Clarke is granted the first divorce in America—from her husband, Denis, who had fathered four children, two by her and two by another woman.

1644

 August 26. A large meteor lights the sky and "causes consternation" among residents of the town.

1645

 August 31. **Roxbury Latin School** is founded by the Rev. John Eliot. Originally called the "Roxburie Free Schoole" (although free only to the sons of its donors), it calls itself "the oldest school in continuous existence in North America" because, unlike Boston Latin, it did not suspend classes during the Revolution. Classes are held in rented rooms until a new school building is constructed in 1652. The school moves several times before arriving at its current location at **101 St. Theresa Avenue** in West Roxbury in 1927.

1646

October 18. * **Rev. John Eliot** preaches to Nonantum chief **Waban** and others of the tribe in today's Brighton. Later known as the "Apostle to the Indians," Eliot reportedly speaks for more than an hour in the Indian language—and is afterwards asked if God will understand prayers offered in the Indian tongue.

1647

 The General Court orders "that every township, after the Lord hath increased them to the number of fifty households, shall appoint one to teach all children to write and read; and when any town shall increase to the number of one hundred families, they shall set up a grammar school, the master thereof to be able to instruct youth so far as they may be fitted for the University." Later called "**The Old Deluder Satan Act**," its purpose is to promote "knowledge of the Scriptures."

1648

June 5. **Margaret Jones** of Charlestown is hanged on **Boston Common** for engaging in witchcraft. A midwife, or lay healer, she had been convicted of putting a fatal spell on a neighbor's cow. She is the first of four women who would be executed for witchcraft in what is today Boston. Twenty people are executed in Salem and 37 people in all of New England. But these numbers pale in comparison to the estimated 30,000 executed for witchcraft in England and Scotland, 75,000 in France, and 100,000 in Germany during the 16th and 17th centuries.

October 18. The General Court allows "the shoomakers of Boston" to "assemble and meet together in Boston at such . . . times as they shall appoynt." The resulting association is considered to be the first labor organization in America.

1649

April. **Solomon Franco** becomes the first Jew to visit Boston. A merchant from Holland, Franco accompanied cargo shipped to Maj. Gen. Edward Gibbons, but becomes embroiled in a dispute over his promised commission, which Gibbons claims should have been paid by the shipper of the goods. Franco is ordered to leave town ("warned out"), and does so soon after.

To prevent fires, the General Court rules that no dwelling "shall be erected and sett up except of stone or bricke, and covered with slate or tyle."

1650

Boston's population is estimated at 2,000.

June 5. The **Second Church in Boston** opens in **North Square**. It is sometimes called the "Church of the Mathers" because its pastors would include **Samuel, Increase,** and **Cotton Mather.** The church burns down on November 26, 1676, and is rebuilt a year later, but is then torn down for firewood by British soldiers in the winter of 1775–1776. The congregation subsequently merges with the First Church in Boston and is today located at **66 Marlborough Street.**

Anne Bradstreet's book of poems, *The Tenth Muse Lately Sprung Up in America,* is published—without her knowledge—by her brother-in-law in London. Considered the first book of poetry by an American author, it is not published in America until 1678, six years after her death.

1651

October 3. To curtail ostentation, the General Court declares: "If a man was not worth 200 pounds, he should not wear gold or silver lace or buttons, nor great boots. Women worth less than 200 pounds are forbidden to wear silk or tiffany hoods or scarfs."

1652

The **Flat Conduit,** a 12-foot-square wooden "reservoir," is built near today's Dock Square. It is the first municipal water supply in the Colonies, with water carried through wooden pipes from nearby springs and used by a small number of subscribers, as well as by the town for fighting fires.

May 31. The General Court orders that no "garbage, dead beast or stinkering things" be deposited on Boston streets.

1653

April 14. The first of Boston's **"Great Fires"** kills three children and destroys eight houses in the area of today's **State** and **Washington Streets**. The town responds by enacting its first fire code. It requires every household to provide a ladder and "a pole of about 12 feet long, with a good large sob at the end of it, to rech to the rofe." The town also appoints a ladder inspector and buys several ladders and "fower strong Iron Crooks" to pull down houses.

1654

May 3. The General Court votes "that the youth thereof be educated, not only in good literature but sound doctrine," but not by teachers "that have manifested themselves unsound in the faith, or scandalous in their lives."

1655

July. **Ann Austin** and **Mary Fisher** become the first Quakers to arrive in Boston. Eight more Quaker women join them in August 1656. All are arrested, jailed, and deported. Soon after, the General Court orders that all Quakers are to have their ears cut off or tongues pierced with a hot iron. A year later, the penalty for being a Quaker is increased—to death.

1656

Bostian Ken is described as the owner of a house and "four acres planted in wheat" in Dorchester. He is believed to be the first African-American property owner in Boston.

August 25. An ordinance is passed prohibiting the galloping of horses in the town. Another ordinance names "the bridge to the North End" as the only place where butchers might "throw their beasts' entrails and garbid, without penalty of a fine."

1657

At the urging of **Rev. John Eliot**, the town of Dorchester sets aside 6,000 acres at **Ponkapoag** as a reservation for the Neponset Indians. It is believed to be the first Indian reservation in the Colonies.

The General Court prohibits the sale of all liquors, "whither knoune by the name of rumme, strong water, wine, strong beere, brandy, cidar, perry, or any other strong liquors, going vnder any other name whatsouer" to the Indians.

1658

At his death, **Stephen Winthrop** leaves a bequest of "fifteene pounds" to be used for the poor. It is the first recorded bequest to the poor in Boston history.

1659

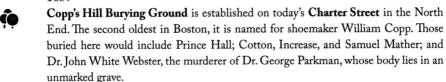

Copp's Hill Burying Ground is established on today's **Charter Street** in the North End. The second oldest in Boston, it is named for shoemaker William Copp. Those buried here would include Prince Hall; Cotton, Increase, and Samuel Mather; and Dr. John White Webster, the murderer of Dr. George Parkman, whose body lies in an unmarked grave.

October 27. Two Quakers, Marmaduke Stevenson and William Robinson, are hanged on **Boston Common**. A third, **Mary Dyer**, is about to be hanged, but her son persuades authorities to spare her. Escorted out of Massachusetts and warned not to return, Dyer does not heed the warning, though, and returns a year later "persuaded that her death was necessary." She is hanged on Boston Common on June 1, 1660.

1660

The **Granary Burying Ground** is established on today's **Tremont Street**. The third oldest in Boston, its graves would include those of: Samuel Adams, the victims of the Boston Massacre, Peter Faneuil, John Hancock, James Otis, Paul Revere, and Elizabeth Foster Vergoose, thought to have been the writer of children's stories "Mother Goose."

1661

(ca.) The **Blake House** is built on today's Massachusetts Avenue (then Cottage Street) in Dorchester. The oldest house in today's Boston, it is later purchased by the city, turned over to the Dorchester Historical Society, and moved approximately four hundred yards to its current location at **735 Columbia Road** in 1895 in one of the first instances of moving an historic building to preserve it.

1662

The **Almshouse** is built at today's **9 Park Street** on Beacon Hill. Although it is originally built as a place for all the town's homeless paupers, eventually a provision is made "for the separation of the vicious from the worthy poor." The building is destroyed by fire in 1682 and rebuilt. The institution is later moved several times—to Leverett Street in 1802, to South Boston in 1825, then to various Boston Harbor islands.

A **General Atherton** is killed on **Boston Common** when his horse collides with a cow. Atherton was on his way home from reviewing his troops. According to an account of the incident, "the cow also suffered."

1663

March 23. The **Great Bridge** opens on today's **Harvard Street**, connecting today's Allston with Cambridge near today's Harvard Square. Swept away by a high tide in 1685, it is rebuilt several times. The current Nicholas Longworth Anderson Bridge opens in 1915.

English naturalist John Josselyn visits Boston. Returning to London, he later writes an account of his visit in which he describes Boston this way: "The town is rich and populous. On the south there is a small, but pleasant, Common, where the Gallants, a little before sunset, walk with their Marmalet-madams, as we do in Morefields, till the nine o'clock bell rings them home to their respective habitations. When presently, the Constables walk their rounds to see good order kept, and to take up the people."

December. John Eliot's complete "Indian Bible," ***Upbiblum God***, is published. The only remaining copy of the book is owned by the Roxbury Latin School and is in the care of Harvard University.

1664

Royal Commissioners from England visit Boston and order that the town stop minting their own money and that citizens say "God Save the King" after the readings of royal proclamations.

1665

July. Captain Richard Davenport, commander of Fort William and Mary on **Castle Island**, is struck and killed by lightning while lying on his cot in the barracks.

The **Lemuel Clap House** is built on Willow Court in Dorchester. Rebuilt in 1765 and enlarged in 1767, it is moved to its current present location at **199 Boston Street** in 1957 and restored thereafter.

1666

Tremont Street is laid out from land along one edge of Boston Common from today's Beacon to today's Boylston Street. It is originally called Common Street.

1667

Jamaica Plain is referred to in an official document as "the Jamaica End of the town of Roxbury." The name "Jamaica Plain" is variously ascribed as being derived from that of the Indian sachem (Cutshamekin) or his wife (Jamaco); a commemoration of Cromwell's victory over Spain in the Caribbean; or from the fact that 17th-century dock workers—or residents—liked to drink their rum (from Jamaica) "neat," or "plain."

1668

Robert Stanton builds the first house in today's **Hyde Park**.

1669

An town ordinance is passed prohibiting rogues, idlers, jugglers, and fiddlers.

1670

Boston is the third busiest port in the British Empire and the leading port in the American colonies.

1671

September 1. English naturalist **John Josselyn** visits Boston and describes "the Inhabitants exceedingly afflicted with griping of the guts, and Feaver, and Ague, and bloody Flux."

1672

Widow and tavern keeper **Alice Thomas** is whipped and then banished for giving "the opportunity to commit carnall wickedness" and for being "a common Baud." She is allowed to return a year later, however, after contributing money for construction of a seawall to protect the harbor.

1673

February 5. The first mail arrives in Boston from New York via the **Boston Post Road**. The beginning of a regular, monthly postal service, the 250-mile trip takes two weeks.

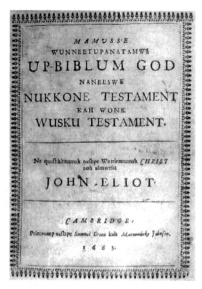

John Eliot's Indian Bible. (Reproduced by permission of the Houghton Library, Harvard University)

1674

September 9. **John Foster** establishes a print shop "at the sign of the Dove" at today's **53 Boylston Street**. The first in Boston, it is allowed only after repeal of the 1638 law confining the printing presses to Cambridge.

1675

June 8. **King Philip's War** begins between the colonists and the Wampanoag Indians. During the war, two-thirds of the settlements in New England are attacked, an estimated 800 European settlers are killed, and an estimated 3,000 Indians are killed. The war ends when Wampanoag leader Metacom (King Philip) is killed in Bridgewater on August 12, 1676. His decapitated and quartered body is brought to Boston for exhibition three days later.

Maurice Brett is found guilty of "filthy carriage." He is sentenced to stand at the gallows with a rope around his neck, receive 39 lashes, and then be banished. When he complains at the severity of the punishment, he is also fined twenty shillings and sentenced to have his ears first nailed to the pillory and then cut off.

1676

May 3. **Mary Rowlandson** of Lancaster arrives in Boston after being freed from captivity by Indians. In a book about her experiences published in 1682, she credits "some Boston gentlewomen and Mr. Usher" for raising the twenty pound ransom she calls "the price of my redemption."

October 2. The **Eliot School** is founded on the site of today's Soldiers Monument at the intersection of today's **Centre** and **South Streets** in Jamaica Plain. The fourth oldest in the U.S., the school receives a contribution from the Rev. John Eliot "for the teaching and instructing of the children of that end of the town (together with such negroes or Indians as may or shall come to said school)." The school moves to its current location at **24 Eliot Street** in 1831 and operates today as the Eliot School of Fine and Applied Arts.

1677

The **Paul Revere House** is built at today's **19 North Square**. The oldest house in Boston Proper today, it is later used for—among other things—a bank and a cigar shop. The building is purchased by Revere's great-grandson in 1902 and reopens as a private museum on April 18, 1908.

January 21. Rev. Thomas Thatcher's *A Brief Rule to guide the Common People of New England How to order themselves and theirs in the Small Pocks, or Measles* is published. The first medical pamphlet published in the Colonies, it is reprinted in 1702.

1678

James Russell builds the first drydock in North America in Charlestown. Its purpose is described as "for taking in of shipps & vessells for repayring vnder water."

Reacting to the growth of intemperate drinking, the Town of Roxbury restricts the sale of wine and liquor to only one "ordinary," or tavern. "This prohibitory enactment," according to Justin Winsor, "did not long remain in force."

1679

The **Province House** is completed at today's **327 Washington Street**. Built by Peter Sargeant, it is the most elaborate home of the day and later serves as the setting for some of Hawthorne's *Twice-Told Tales* and as the royal governor's mansion. Sold in 1796, it later becomes a tavern and a dance hall. Despite efforts to preserve it, the building is demolished in 1922.

1680

The **Old Feather Store** is built in **Dock Square**. Built by Thomas Stanbury, it becomes a Boston landmark, known for its gabled roof and rough plaster walls. The building is torn down in 1860.

The **Green Dragon Tavern** opens at today's **84 Union Street**. Originally a private home built in 1657, it is one of the earliest taverns in Boston and becomes a popular meeting place, first for Masonic groups, then for Colonists resisting British rule. The building is torn down in 1828. A tavern with the same name is located today at **11 Marshall Street**.

1681

The **Barricado** is completed along the route of today's Atlantic Avenue. A 2,200-foot-long breakwater, it is built as a defense against possible attack by the Dutch or French, but proves unnecessary and soon falls into disrepair.

July 22. A child is killed when the Roxbury homes of Joshua Lamb and a neighbor burn down. It is subsequently discovered later that the fire was set by a slave called "Black Maria." She is executed on Boston Common on October 2, 1681. "The severity of the sentence," historian Robert Twombly later writes, "can be attributed to the death and to public hysteria over a rash of conflagrations set by servants of several races in and around Boston."

1682

May 12. A baby born two days after his father's death is named **Fathergone Dinely**.

Increase Mather's *Heaven's Alarm to the World* is published. In it, he contends that the appearance of Halley's Comet this year is a sign of God's displeasure with the world.

1683

November 7. The General Court passes an ordinance declaring: "Henceforth no Dwelling-house, Warehouse, Shop, Barn, Stable, or any other Housing (in Boston), shall be Erected and set up in Boston, except of Stone or Brick." The law is generally ignored.

The *New England Primer* is first published by Benjamin Harris at the London Coffee House. The first schoolbook printed in America, it includes the prayer "Now I Lay Me Down to Sleep." The book is later estimated to have sold more than 5 million copies.

1684

A "free writing school" opens in today's Scollay Square. The town's first, it is established to teach boys unable to attend the Latin School. The writing schools are first open to girls—from April 20 to October 20 only—in 1789.

October 23. The British Parliament revokes the Massachusetts Bay Colony charter on the grounds that the colony has not upheld English laws or shown sufficient deference to Charles II.

1685

March 19. Town meeting appoints a committee to purchase any claim "legal or pretended" by Indians to "Deare Island, the Necke of Boston, or any parte thereof." Historians later speculate that the action is taken to protect property owners in light of the revocation of the Massachusetts Bay charter by the British Parliament.

November 5. The first annual **Pope's Night** is celebrated in Boston. Held on the anniversary of Guy Fawkes Day (November 5, 1605), the festivities included a parade and a battle between groups of residents from the North and South Ends who fight to capture and burn each other's effigies of the pope. The "celebration" becomes more and more violent and is celebrated officially for the last time in 1774.

1686

December 20. **Sir Edmund Andros** arrives in Boston as royal governor of the newly created Dominion of New England. He imposes new taxes, forces landowners to pay a fee to retain their land, and declares that he considers Indian signatures on land titles

to be "of no more worth than the scratch of a bear paw."

1687

In the annual town election, only "freemen"—those with a taxable estate of at least 80 pounds—are eligible to vote. There are only 24 such freemen in the town.

March 25. The first Anglican service in Boston is held at the First Church, then at today's **201 Washington Street**. It is held by order of Gov. Andros, who demands use of one of the existing Congregational churches by the "Established Church."

1688

November 16. **Mary "Goody" Glover** is hanged on **Boston Common**. The fourth and last person to be executed for witchcraft in Boston, she had been accused by the 13-year-old daughter of her mistress after Glover had scolded the girl. Glover was convicted party because of her inability to recite the Lord's Prayer in English, which she knew only in Latin. Her last words are reportedly, "I die a Catholic."

1689

April 18. After news reaches Boston that James II has been deposed and William and Mary of Orange have succeeded him to the throne, residents depose Gov. Edmund Andros in what is later called the "**Bloodless Revolution**." They imprison Andros at Castle Island and subsequently send him back to England.

1690

The first paper money issued in America is printed in Boston from plates engraved by **John Cony**. The money is used to pay the soldiers who took part in the unsuccessful attack on Quebec.

September 25. The first issue of ***Publick Occurrences: Both Foreign and Domestic*** appears. The first newspaper in the Colonies, it is published by **Benjamin Harris** at the London Coffee House and banned four days later for printing "sundry doubtful and uncertain Reports." All remaining copies are then destroyed, and the only copy known to exist today is in the British Library.

1691

October 7. A new charter is issued by William III that joins the Massachusetts Bay, Plymouth, and Maine Colonies into the Royal Province of Massachusetts Bay. Under its terms, the king appoints the governor and the people elect 28 councillors (18 from Massachusetts, four of these from Boston). The new charter also removes religious requirements for officeholders and guarantees religious tolerance for all—except Catholics.

1692

May. Lieutenant Governor **William Stoughton** of Dorchester and **Samuel Sewall** of Boston are appointed to the special Court of Oyer and Terminer to preside over the witchcraft trials in Salem. Reflecting on the role he played as one of the judges in the Salem witchcraft trials, Samuel Sewall later writes in his diary: "I take the blame and shame."

1693

Cotton Mather's *The Wonders of the Invisible World* is published, adding to the witchcraft hysteria. Poet Robert Lowell later describes Mather as "a power-crazed mind, bent on destroying darkness with darkness."

1694

Hannah Newell is convicted of "Adultery by her owne confession." She is sentenced to receive "Fifteen stripes Severally to be laid on upon her naked back at the Common Whipping post." Her lover, Lambert Despar, is given 25 lashes and sentenced to "stand upon the Pillory for the space of the full hower with Adultery in Capitall letters written upon his brest."

1695

The list of Boston residents includes one described only as **"Samuel the Jew."**

1696

The General Court passes a law creating a regulated, public market in Boston, which is one of the few towns without one. The selectmen subsequently order that the town market operate on Tuesday, Thursday, and Saturday.

1697

The winter of 1697–1698 is described as "the terriblest winter of the century."

1698

The first road map to be printed for public use in America appears in Tulley's *Almanack*. The map includes a list of towns, roads and distances from Boston, as well as a list of tavern keepers in the area.

Kissing is declared "a fineable offense (if caught)."

1699

July 6. **Captain Kidd** is arrested for piracy at a house near today's corner of **Washington** and **Milk Streets** on a warrant issued by Royal Governor Lord Bellomont, who had been part of a group who had hired Kidd to hunt pirates in Africa. Kidd is imprisoned, shipped to England, tried, found guilty, and hanged—and his body is placed on a gibbet and left to rot.

1700 – 1799

1700

Boston's population is estimated at 6,700.

June 12. Samuel Sewall's ***The Selling of Joseph: A Memorial*** is published. The first anti-slavery tract to appear in the Colonies, it contains the passage: [Liberty is]"the real value unto life; none ought to part with it themselves or deprive others of it but upon mature Consideration." There are an estimated 400 slaves in Boston at this time, almost double the number there had been in 1676. A year later, selectmen vote to ask their representatives at the General Court to "put a period to negroes being slaves."

1701

When **Increase Mather** is appointed president of **Harvard College**, he moves from Boston to Cambridge to comply with the residency requirement for the position. But he soon resigns and moves back to Boston, explaining: "Should I leave off preaching to 1500 souls. . . only to expound to forty or fifty Children, a few of them capable of edification by such Exercises?"

1702

May 28. News of the death of **King William III** and accession of **Queen Anne** is marked by a 21-gun salute in Boston.

1703

The HMS *Hazard* runs aground and sinks off **Georges Island**.

1704

April 19. Selectmen authorize the expenditure of 100 pounds to pave those streets in Boston judged "most needful, having particular regard to the hiway right to old Mrs. Stoddard's house."

April 24. The first issue of the ***Boston News-Letter*** appears. Boston's second newspaper and the first to publish regularly in the Colonies, the one-sheet weekly is published by postmaster John Campbell from his shop at today's **268 Washington Street**.

1705

November 13. The settlement known as Muddy River is set off from Boston and becomes the **Town of Brookline**.

1706

May. The votes to erect a **Powder House** on **Boston Common**. Guarded at all times by two men, a watch house is also built on the adjacent hill. Town meeting later votes to remove it in 1750, concluding: "the town will do nothing concerning it."

Cotton Mather's *The Negro Christianized* is published. In it he describes as "Men, and not Beasts, that you have bought."

1707

A group of businessmen led by **Elisha Cooke** agrees to widen the road on Boston Neck in return for development rights to the property. The town agrees—on condition that the group erects barriers to "secure and keep off the sea." According to historian G.B. Warden, Cooke, a Harvard graduate, physician, and landlord, "perhaps did more for Boston than any other man in the eighteenth century, including the heroes of the Revolutionary generation."

1708

May 3. The task of naming each of the town's 110 streets, lanes, and alleys is completed.

March 14. A committee is formed to "draft a charter of incorporation" for "the better government of the town." But for more than 100 years the town regularly votes against applying for a charter as a city. **Josiah Quincy** later criticizes that, among other problems with the town meeting form of government, was that "those only who obtained places near the moderator could even hear the discussion. A few busy or interested individuals easily obtained the management of the most important affairs in an assembly in which the greater number could have neither voice nor hearing."

1709

February. A **Great Tide** occurs, flooding wharves, cellars, and the lower floors of houses and warehouses around the docks.

1710

April. Due to a food shortage, a mob attacks a ship owned by merchant **Andrew Belcher** that is about to leave Boston Harbor with a load of grain bound for the Caribbean. Their complaint, according to historian Gary Nash, is that Belcher, "chose to export grain to the Caribbean, at a handsome profit, rather than sell it for a smaller profit to hungry townspeople."

1711

The **Moses Pierce–Hichborn** house is built, adjacent to the Paul Revere House, at **19 North Square** in the North End. One of the oldest brick houses in Boston, a police raid on an illegal gambling operation there in 1948 sparks the successful effort to preserve the building.

October 2. The **Great Fire of 1711** burns more than one-third of the town. The blaze destroys a hundred buildings in the Cornhill area, including the Town House, the First Church, and the Third Church. The fire prompts establishment of fire wards, each with a warden responsible for putting out fires, and volunteer fire companies, which compete to be first on the scene since their only pay comes in the form of goods salvaged from fires.

The State House, ca. 1794. Watercolor by unknown artist. (Courtesy of the Bostonian Society)

1712

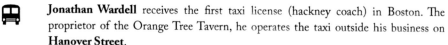

Jonathan Wardell receives the first taxi license (hackney coach) in Boston. The proprietor of the Orange Tree Tavern, he operates the taxi outside his business on **Hanover Street**.

The **Bunch of Grapes Tavern** opens at today's **53 State Street**. It is built on the site of the Castle Tavern, which had been renamed the Bunch of Grapes in 1658, and burned down in the Great Fire of 1711. The new building is torn down to make way for construction of the New England Bank in 1798.

1713

May 5. The **Old State House** is dedicated at today's **206 Washington Street**. A replacement for the original Town House (built in 1657 and destroyed by the Great Fire of 1711), it is the oldest public building in Boston and the second oldest in the U.S. after the governor's palace in Santa Fe. The building contains a merchant's hall on the first floor, and court and council chambers on the second floor. A visitors' gallery, the first in any legislative assembly in the world, is added in 1767. The building is saved from being purchased by the city of Chicago and moved to the "Windy City" when the **Bostonian Society** is founded to purchase and restore the building in 1881.

1714

(ca.) The **Capen House** is built at **41 Union Street**. The building serves as headquarters of Ebenezer Hancock, paymaster of the Colonial army, during the Revolutionary War. The Duke of Chartres lives on the second floor during the French Revolution, earning his living by giving French lessons, before returning to France to become King Louis Philippe in 1830. Isaiah Thomas publishes the *Massachusetts Spy* on the third floor from 1771 to 1775. The building becomes home of the **Union Oyster House** restaurant in 1826.

1715

Long Wharf is completed. The longest pier in the Colonies, it is extended to more than 1,700 feet long and over 100 feet wide in 1826, with a 30-foot roadway down its center and lined on both sides with warehouses and shops.

1716

September 14. **Boston Light** goes into service on **Little Brewster Island**. The first lighthouse built in North America, it is the oldest continuously operated and occupied lighthouse in the U.S. The lighthouse is automated in 1998, but a Coast Guard crew remains there to perform other duties.

1717

September 28. Selectmen warn recently arrived Irish immigrant **James Goodwin** to leave Boston, in the first recorded instance of the town discouraging Irish immigrants.

February 27. **The Great Snow** begins. The storm lasts for more than a week and adds six feet to the total snowfall for the winter, which reaches as much as 10 or 20 feet in some parts of New England. Cotton Mather writes: "As mighty a snow, as perhaps has been known in the memory of Man, is at this Time lying on the Ground."

1718

October 11. The **Boston Mutual Fire Society** is established. The first private fire aid organization in America, it is made up of 20 members who agree to fight any fires that strike one another's property.

1719

December 17. The appearance of the aurora borealis is first recorded in Boston. The flashing lights in the night sky alarm many residents, some assuming they portend the end of the world.

1720

When the **Rev. Peter Thatcher** is installed as the minister of the New North Church at today's **401 Hanover Street** in the North End, members of the congregation express their displeasure, according to historian Walter Muir Whitehill, "by pissing over the railing onto the heads of those below."

1721

June 26. **Dr. Zabdiel Boylston** introduces inoculation to combat smallpox in Boston. After Boylston administers the vaccine to his six-year-old son, his "negro man Jack," and a "negro boy, of 2½, a number of residents agree to the treatment. Opponents of the procedure nearly lynch Boylston, but it proves to be successful. While over 800 people die from this latest outbreak of the disease, only six of the nearly 250 people that Boylston inoculates succumb to it.

1722

John Bonner's *The Town of Boston in New England* is published. The first detailed

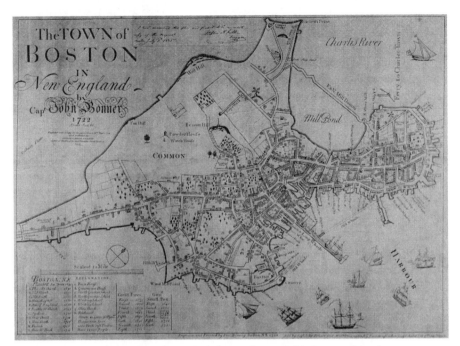

"The Town of Boston in New England" by Capt. John Bonner, 1722. (Courtesy of the Bostonian Society)

map of the town, the *Boston News-Letter* describes it as "A Curious Ingraven Map of the Town of Boston, with all of the streets, lanes, Alleys, Wharffs & Houses, the Like never done before."

April 2. **Benjamin Franklin**'s first article appears in the *New England Courant* published on today's **Court Street**. The article appears under the byline Silence Dogood. A year later, the now 17-year-old Franklin breaks the indenture agreement with his brother and runs away to Philadelphia.

1723

December 29. Christ Church (**Old North Church**) is dedicated at **193 Salem Street** in the North End. Designed by William Price, it is the oldest church building in today's Boston. The steeple is added in 1740. The church bells, cast in England in 1744 and hung by Paul Revere in 1754, are the oldest in the Colonies. The steeple is first toppled by the Great Gale in 1804, and then by Hurricane Carol in 1954.

1724

A Pacificatory Letter about Psalmody, or Singing of Psalms is published as an anonymous letter. In it, the author attempts to mediate the dispute raging in pulpits throughout the town between continued use of the "old way of singing" (unaccompanied by music and led by a deacon) or adoption of the more modern way (with music and led by a singing master).

1725

Daniel Neal's *History of New England* is published in London. In it, he writes: "A Gentleman from London would almost think himself at home at Boston, when he observes the numbers of people, their Houses, their Furniture, their Tables, their Dress and Conversation, which, perhaps, is as splendid and showy, as that of the most considerable Tradesmen in London."

1726

June 12. Pirates **Samuel Cole, Henry Grenville**, and **William Fly** are hanged on Boston Common. The first two are buried at Nix's Mate, a small outcropping in Boston Harbor. Fly's body is hung in chains there—as a warning to passing sailors against involvement in piracy.

1727

October 29. Residents of Boston are awakened by an earthquake. The sound is described as "horrid rumbling, like the noise of many coaches together driving on the paved stones," and is said to have been felt through "the whole country north of the Delaware River."

1728

July 3. After an argument in the **Royal Exchange Tavern** at today's **28 State Street**, Henry Phillips kills his friend Benjamin Woodbridge in a duel on **Boston Common**. Phillips subsequently flees to France. Woodbridge is buried in the Granary Burying Ground. To discourage future duels, a town ordinance is passed requiring the victor in duels "to be imprisoned 12 months without bail," and the vanquished to be buried "near the usual place of public execution with a stake driven through the body."

1729

The **Federal Street Church** begins meeting in a converted barn on Long Lane at today's **145 Federal Street**. The building is replaced on the same site by one designed by Charles Bulfinch in 1744. Originally Presbyterian, the congregation becomes Congregational in 1780, then Unitarian in 1786. **William Ellery Channing** serves as pastor from 1803 to 1842. The church moves to what becomes known as the Arlington Street Church at **351 Boylston Street** in 1861.

1730

September. Boston celebrates the town's 100th anniversary with a "Jubilee," which consists of orations delivered at various churches. Some sort of jubilee celebration is held every 50 years from this time forward.

April 26. The **Old South Meeting House** (originally Third Church in Boston) opens on the former site of John Winthrop's garden at today's **310 Washington Street**. A replacement for the original church, built in 1669, it is for many years the town's largest hall. The building is damaged by British soldiers, who use it as a riding rink and stable during the Siege of Boston. When the congregation moves to a new building in the Back Bay in 1875, it is saved from demolition by an effort that Walter Muir Whitehill later describes as "the first instance in Boston where respect for the historical and architectural heritage of the city triumphed over considerations of profit, expediency, laziness and vulgar convenience."

 The first art exhibit is held in Boston, a display of the painting of Scottish-born artist **John Smibart**. Smibart is the foremost portrait painter in town at the time—working, according to art historian Arthur Dexter, in "A Puritan society (which) was not favorable to art."

Old North Church (Christ Church, Salem Street). Engraving by Dearborn for The History of Boston. (Courtesy of the Bostonian Society)

1731

The first recorded publicly announced musical concert in the Colonies—other than for sacred music—is held in the home of a Dr. Noyes in **Dock Square**.

1732

Town officials are alarmed at a rumor that a Catholic priest is in the area and that he is planning to say a Mass somewhere on March 17, which is described as "what they call St. Patrick's Day."

1733

British Parliament passes The **Molasses Act**, taxing its import from the West Indies. The law is subsequently rescinded but then re-enacted. It is particularly disruptive to the "molasses, rum, and slaves" triangle that has become so important to Boston's economy.

July 30. The **Provincial Grand Lodge of Masons in Massachusetts** is organized at the Bunch of Grapes Tavern at today's **53 State Street**. The first Masonic lodge in America, it is later named the St. John's Lodge. Early members include Sam Adams, John Hancock, Paul Revere, and Joseph Warren.

1734

June 4. After the town finally approves their construction, markets are opened at North Square, Dock Square, and the South End. But the Dock Square market is destroyed three years later by members of a mob, dressed as clergymen, who are protesting the high, regulated prices being charged there.

1735

August 15. **Trinity Church** opens at today's **16 Summer Street**. It was founded "by

Faneuil Hall, 1775. Engraving by C.B. Hall in Massachusetts Magazine. (Courtesy of the Bostonian Society)

reason that the (King's) Chapel is full and no pews are to be bought by newcomers." The building is replaced by a larger church in 1829. The current church in the Back Bay is built in 1877.*

1736

After the brigantine *Bootle*, sailing from Cork, anchors in **Boston Harbor**, the ship's captain, **Robert Boyd,** is summoned before town authorities and made to promise not to allow any of his passengers to "come on Shaor."

1737

The **Thomas Hancock House** is built at today's **29 Beacon Street** overlooking Boston Common. The granite mansion is home of its wealthiest merchant and is later inherited by his nephew, John Hancock. Despite one of the first efforts at preservation in Boston history, the house is torn down in 1863.

April 13. The **Boston Stone** is inserted into the wall of a building at **9 Marshall Street**. A piece of granite originally brought from England by Thomas Child for grinding paint, it is used to protect the facade from passing vehicles. A neighbor then proposes that it be used like the London Stone—as a point from which distances to Boston are measured. The stone is later transferred into the base of the building that currently occupies the site.

1738

The **Town Workhouse** "for the idle and dissolute poor" opens at today's **5 Park Street** on Beacon Hill. A **House of Industry** "for the unfortunate poor" opens in South Boston in 1825.

1739

John Colman establishes the first private bank in Boston. Its directors include Samuel Adams. The bank is closed a year later when Parliament prohibits the issuance of paper money in the Colonies.

1740

Boston's population peaks at an estimated 17,000, a figure that is not exceeded for another 50 years.

October 12. Revivalist Methodist minister **George Whitefield** ends his month-long crusade in Boston by preaching to a crowd on **Boston Common** estimated at 30,000 people—nearly twice the population of the town. It is described later as the high point of the "Great Awakening." Some of those attending are later treated by physicians and diagnosed as "Rendered insane by listening to Rev. Whitefield."

1741

October 16. The **First Corps of Cadets** is chartered as the bodyguard for Massachusetts governors. Except during the period from 1774 to 1786, it continues to serve that capacity today.

1742

September 16. **Faneuil Hall** opens by hosting its first public meeting. Designed by John Smibart, the wooden building includes a first-floor market and a second floor that serves as the town hall. According to some sources, the grasshopper weathervane above the building is a symbol from the Faneuil family crest; according to others, it is done in imitation of a practice by British banks. Later dubbed the "Cradle of Liberty," the building is rebuilt in brick and enlarged by Charles Bulfinch in 1806.

1743

Boston bakers engage in the first strike in the town's history. They refuse to bake bread until they are allowed to increase their prices—which, unlike other professions of the time, are regulated by the government.

1744

The **Parting Stone** is erected in **John Eliot Square** in Roxbury. Placed there by Chief Justice Paul Dudley, it marks the spot where the Post Road branches north to Cambridge and Watertown and south to Dedham and Rhode Island.

1745

Joseph Bennett, a visiting Englishman, describes how Boston ladies "visit, drink tea and indulge every piece of gentility to the height of the mode, and neglect the affairs of their families with as good a grace as the first ladies in London."

1746

September 22. Members of town meeting vote to appoint a committee to make "strict

Search and enquiry" into the actions of local Catholics to make sure they do not pose a danger to the town.

1747

(ca.) The **Shirley-Eustis House** is built for Royal Governor William Shirley at today's **33 Shirley Street** in Roxbury. Designed by Peter Harrison, it is used by the Colonists as a barracks and hospital during the Revolution and later becomes the home of Dr. William Eustis, governor of the Commonwealth of Massachusetts from 1823 to 1825. The building was saved by preservationists in 1913 and is today a museum.

November 17. The **Impressment Riot** breaks out when a mob attacks British sailors from the warship *Preston* who are attempting to force merchant seamen to serve in the English Navy. Several British officers are seized, three days of rioting follow, and Governor Shirley is forced to take refuge at Castle William. The officers are eventually released and the British fleet leaves Boston.

1748

March 14. An advertisement in the *Boston Post-Boy* announces publication of "*A Treatis, proving* (a Posteriori) *that most of the Disorders incident to the* Fair Sex, *are owing to* Flatulencies *not seasonally vented.*" The ad is a reprint of a spoof published three years earlier in London, although with a less scatological title.

1749

October 17. **Samuel Adams** marries **Elizabeth Checkley** in a service officiated by her father, the Rev. Samuel Checkley at the New South Church on Church Green off today's **Summer Street**.

1750

March. Thomas Otway's ***The Orphan—or Unhappy Marriage*** is performed in the British Coffee House at today's **66 State Street**. The first play performed in Boston, its production prompts the General Court to pass a law prohibiting plays "tending to increase immortality, impiety and contempt of religion." The law is not repealed until 1797.

1751

May 17. A man described only as "a young negro" is hanged on **Boston Common** for murder.

1752

January to August. The town's longest smallpox epidemic occurs. Selectmen later report that 514 of the 5,544 stricken die, but only 31 of the 2,109 who were inoculated were among those who succumbed to the disease.

1753

Benjamin Franklin returns to Boston in his capacity as Colonial postmaster to lay out the mile markers along the Boston Post Road. Riding in a carriage and using a homemade odometer attached to the wheel, he marks the distances along the 250-mile route through Worcester, Springfield, Hartford, and New Haven to New York.

1754

August 11. **King's Chapel** opens at today's **58 Tremont Street**. A replacement for the original chapel (built in 1689), it is designed by Peter Harrison and the exterior is made from the first granite taken from quarries in Quincy. The church's pulpit is the oldest in continuous use in the U.S. A steeple is never erected due to lack of funds. British officers worship here during the Siege of Boston, and it becomes the first Unitarian church in Boston in 1787.

1755

May 2. Three ships sail from Boston to Acadia, Maine, carrying settlers who refuse to swear allegiance to England. **Henry Wadsworth Longfellow** later immortalizes their expulsion in his poem "**Evangeline.**"

November 18. An earthquake shakes Boston for more than four minutes. It occurs 17 days after the Lisbon earthquake and is the last major earthquake to strike New England. Tremors topple ten chimneys and the weather vane on Faneuil Hall and cause old springs to dry up and new springs to flow.

1756

February. **George Washington** makes his first visit to Boston, staying for two weeks at the Cromwell's Head Inn at today's **17 School Street**. The purpose of his visit is to have Gov. Shirley, the commander-in-chief of American militia forces, confirm that Washington, a colonel in Virginia, outranks a captain in Maryland.

1757

September 13. Daredevil **John Childs**, wearing leather wings, slides down a rope stretched from the steeple of the Old North Church at today's **193 Salem Street** in the North End. He repeats the feat a second time, while firing two pistols during his descent. The stunt attracts such a large crowd that the town's Selectmen order him to stop.

1758

November 16. **John Adams** and **Samuel Quincy** are sworn into the Suffolk County bar and allowed to practice law. But during this year, **Benjamin Austin**, a leader of Boston's artisans and friend of Samuel Adams, publishes a series of articles in which he attacks lawyers and the existing legal code. "It has become necessary for the welfare and security of the Commonwealth that this order of men should be ANNHILLATED," he writes.

1759

A marriage advertisement appears in the *Boston Evening Post* that reads: "OBJECT (WE HOPE) MATRIMONY. To the Ladies. Any young Lady between the Age of Eighteen and twenty three of a Midling Stature; brown Hair, regular Features and a Lively Brisk Eye: Of Good Morals & not Tinctured with anything that may Sully so

Distinguishable a Form possessed of 3 or 400 pounds entirely her own Disposal and where there will be no necessity of going Through the tiresome Talk of addressing Parents or Guardians for their consent." Those interested in responding to the advertisement are advised to contact "A.W. at the British Coffee House in King Street" and are assured that "Profound Secrecy will be observ'd."

1760

The **Loring-Greenough House** is completed at **12 South Street** in Jamaica Plain. Built for British Navy Commander Joshua Loring, it serves as headquarters for Gen. Nathaniel Greene during the Siege of Boston, then becomes the first military hospital in Boston. The building is moved in 1851 and is later owned by the Greenough family. It is purchased by the Tuesday Club, a women's literary society, in 1924, saved from demolition, and operates as a museum today.

1761

February 24. **James Otis** denounces the Writs of Assistance in a fiery, four-hour speech before the court at the Old State House (then known as the Town House) at today's **206 Washington Street**. The recently passed laws enable customs officials to search houses and warehouses for smuggled goods. In his speech, Otis uses the phrase "taxation without representation." John Adams later writes: "Otis was a flame of fire . . . then and there the child independence was born."

1762

A group that includes **Samuel Adams, James Otis,** and possibly **Paul Revere** begins to meet secretly in the Long Room above the shop of the *Boston Gazette* on today's **Court Street**.

1763

British Parliament passes the first of the **Grenville Acts**. The Proclamation Act prohibits Colonists from crossing the Appalachian Mountains and settling in the Ohio Valley. The Currency Act prohibits Colonists from coining money or issuing currency. The Sugar Act, passed a year later, imposes duties on goods imported into America, including molasses and sugar.

1764

John Mein establishes the London Bookstore at today's **60 State Street**. The first circulating library in Boston, it operates with Mein selling subscriptions for the right to use of his personal library of more than a thousand volumes."

November 5. During the annual **Pope's Night** celebration, a five-year-old boy is run over and killed by a wagon carrying a float that contains an effigy of the pope. Samuel Smith, a ship carpenter and leader of the North End crowd, and Ebenezer MacIntosh, a leather worker and leader of the South End crowd, are indicted for causing the fatal accident. However, the two men are never brought to trial.

1765

August 14. The **Liberty Tree** is "consecrated" at the corner of today's **Washington** and **Essex Streets** when members of a group calling themselves the "**Sons of Liberty**" gather to protest enactment by the British Parliament of the Stamp Act, which requires the purchase of government stamps for all legal documents and newspapers printed in the Colonies. The rebels hang an effigy of Boston stamp distributor Andrew Oliver and then attack Oliver's office and house, prompting him to resign his post a few months later. The Liberty Tree stands for another 10 years until it is chopped down for firewood by British troops in August 1775. Legend has it that one of the soldiers is killed when the tree falls.

Boston-born John Singleton Copley completes his painting **Henry Pelham** *(Boy with a Squirrel)*. After being shown later in London, Benjamin West declares its coloring the equal of Titian.

1766

May 19. The official notice of the repeal of the Stamp Act is proclaimed from the balcony of the Old State House at today's **206 Washington Street**, prompting the ringing of church bells, firing of guns, and the setting off of fireworks.

May 26. Town meeting votes to request of Boston's representatives at the General Court "That for the total abolishing of slavery among us, That you move for a law to prohibit the importation and purchasing of slaves for the future."

1767

Phillis Wheatley publishes her first poem, "On Messrs. Hussey and Coffin," in the *Newport Mercury*. It is the first poem published by an African-American in the Colonies. Wheatley is a 15-year-old slave, working in the home of Mrs. Susanna Wheatley on today's **State Street**, who arrived in Boston seven years before from Senegal.

1768

June 10. **John Hancock**'s sloop, *Liberty*, carrying a cargo of wine, is seized on its return from Madeira. Hancock is charged with smuggling for not paying the duties imposed by the Townshend Acts. His arrest prompts the so-called "**Liberty Riot**" two days later, when a crowd of 1500 people gather at **Clark's Wharf** in the North End.

October 1. The **Occupation of Boston** begins. Twelve hundred troops from 12 ships recently arrived in Boston Harbor come ashore at **Long Wharf** "with drums beating and fifes playing"—in what is later described as an attempt "to overawe the inhabitants" of Boston. As historian G.B. Warden later writes: "No Bostonian could ever forget the strange, unwanted sight of scarlet uniforms against the grays and browns of the narrow streets and wooden houses. For every soldier who marched off Long Wharf that day, one Bostonian began to wonder whether allegiance to England was really worth such a travesty, whether the town and the colonies might well do better to be independent than to tolerate such a horrid miscarriage of justice, such an unsettling reversal of peacetime values."

1769

August 1. Royal Governor **Sir Francis Bernard**, who had long been asking to be recalled to London, sails for England on board the *Rippon*, leaving Thomas Hutchinson as acting governor. In a letter written on September 20, he writes: "If we could keep off the influence of Boston for one twelve-month, I think we could bring the rest of the province to their senses."

1770

March 5. The **Boston Massacre** takes place near the site of today's **60 State Street**. After a crowd pelts British sentry Hugh White with snowballs and other missiles, Captain Thomas Preston and seven British soldiers intervene to defend White. The crowd taunts the soldiers, more missiles are thrown, and the soldiers open fire—even though Preston later denies giving the order to do so. Five colonists are killed: **Crispus Attucks**, a runaway slave from Framingham; **Samuel Gray**, a rope worker; **James Caldwell**, a seaman; 17-year-old **Samuel Maverick**; and **Patrick Carr**, an Irish tailor. All five are buried at the Granary Burying Ground on **Tremont Street**.

October 30. After a trial in which he is defended by **Josiah Quincy Jr.** and **John Adams**, Captain Preston is acquitted of charges involving his conduct in the recent "massacre." Six of his soldiers are also subsequently acquitted. Two are convicted of manslaughter but escape the death sentences by pleading "benefit of clergy," and are punished instead by being branded with the letter M (for murderer) on their left thumbs. All of the soldiers are then sent back to England.

1771

March 5. **James Lovell** delivers the first **Boston Massacre Oration**. When Faneuil Hall proves too small for the crowd, the ceremony is moved to the Old South Meeting House at today's **310 Washington Street**. The annual speeches on this date continue until replaced by an annual July 4 oration beginning in 1783.

February 8. The first large orchestra concert in Boston is held at the Concert Hall on **Hanover Street**. Organized by Josiah Flagg, it features the 64th Regiment Military Band playing selections including those by J. C. Bach and Handel.

1772

November 2. At town meeting in Faneuil Hall, **Samuel Adams** moves to create a 21-member "committee of correspondence." The purpose of this committee, according to Adams, is "to state the rights of the Colonists and of this Province in particular" and "to communicate and publish the same to the several towns in this province and to the world." The committee is created and its subsequent report, accepted at town meeting on November 20, 1772, helps provide the framework for the Declaration of Independence and the First Amendment of the Constitution. Gov. Hutchinson later calls it a "declaration of Independency," and 600 copies are printed and sent to the selectmen of each town in the province.

1773

May 10. British Parliament passes the **Tea Act**, which allows the struggling East India

The Bloody Massacre. *Engraving by Paul Revere, 1770.* (Courtesy of the Bostonian Society)

Company to sell its surplus tea directly to the Colonies. Even though, as Governor Hutchinson points out, "the poor people in America drank the same tea in quality at three shillings a pound which people in England drank at six shillings," Colonists resent the tax and Boston merchants resent that the only "consignees" in the town allowed to sell tea are all relatives or friends of Governor Hutchinson.

October 28. The *Dartmouth*, loaded with 114 chests of East India Company tea, arrives in Boston Harbor. The *Eleanor* and the *Beaver* arrives some weeks later.

December 16. The **Boston Tea Party** is held. Thousands of residents meet first at Faneuil Hall and then at the Old South Meeting House and vote to ask Governor Hutchinson to send the three tea ships back to England without unloading their cargo. When Hutchinson refuses, a group of approximately 50 men, crudely disguised as Indians, proceeds from the Old South Meeting House to Griffin's Wharf at today's **470 Atlantic Avenue** and dumps 342 chests of tea—worth more than $1 million in today's dollars—into Boston Harbor.

1774

March 25. British Parliament passes the **Coercive Acts**. They include the Boston Port Bill, which closes the port of Boston until the East India Company and customs office are reimbursed for their losses as a result of the Boston Tea Party; the Regulating Act, which revokes the Massachusetts charter; and the Quartering Act, which allowed troops to be housed in private homes.

May 17. **General Thomas Gage** is appointed royal governor and replaces the civilian government of the Massachusetts Bay Colony with a military one. In England, Edmund Burke later declares: "The cause of Boston is become the cause of all America. By these acts of oppression, you have made Boston the Lord Mayor of America."

1775

April 18. **Paul Revere's Ride** takes place. Sexton Robert Newman hangs two lamps in the tower of the Old North Church to signal that British troops are being ferried across Boston Harbor en route to seize military supplies stored in Lexington and Concord. But the signal is for the approximately 40 other riders. Revere himself is rowed across the harbor to Charlestown at the same time as the British troops. He rides from there to Lexington but is detained by British soldiers before he can reach Concord. The **Battles of Lexington** and **Concord** are fought the next day, initiating the Revolutionary War.

April 19. **Boston Latin School** suspends classes, with headmaster **John Lovell** reportedly announcing: "War's begun and school's done; *deponite libros*." Lovell, a Loyalist, later sails for Halifax when the British evacuate Boston. His son **James Lovell**, the school's assistant headmaster, sails for Halifax, too—but, since he is a Patriot, he goes as a prisoner.

April 20. The **Siege of Boston** begins when Colonial troops surround the town. The British are virtual captives and set up their headquarters at the British Coffee House at today's **66 State Street**.

June 17. The **Battle of Bunker Hill** is fought on neighboring **Breed's Hill** in Charlestown. Although the British are ultimately victorious, they suffer twice the number of casualties as the Colonial forces, led by General Israel Putnam and Colonel William Prescott. Prescott may or may not have said "Don't fire until you see the whites of their eyes," a well-known military command at the time. But he did say "Show the bastards. You show them." During and after the battle, the British burn down most of the 500 structures in Charlestown.

1776

March 4. Under cover of darkness, Colonial forces seize **Dorchester Heights** in today's South Boston and train the cannons brought by Henry Knox from Fort Ticonderoga on the town of Boston and on the British fleet in Boston Harbor.

March 17. The **Evacuation of Boston** takes place, as the British surrender the town. Approximately 9,000 British troops and 1,000 Loyalists board 125 ships in Boston harbor, sailing eventually for Halifax, Nova Scotia.

July 18. At 1 p.m., the ***Declaration of Independence*** is first read in Boston at the Old State House at today's **206 Washington Street**. In the celebration that follows, the carved figures of the lion and unicorn, symbols of English rule, are torn down from the walls of the building and burnt in a bonfire—along with the signs from King's Arms, the Royal Coffee House, and street signs from King and Queen Streets. Replicas of the lion and unicorn ornaments are once more affixed to the Old State House in 1992.

1777

May 26. Despite the upheaval of the Revolution, town meeting declines to vote to form a new town government in Boston, declaring that "a suitable time will properly come before the people at large to delegate a select number for that purpose, and that alone."

Engraving of Phillis Wheatley from the frontispiece of Poems on Various Subjects, Religious and Moral, by Phillis Wheatley, Negro Servant to Mr. John Wheatley, of Boston, in New England. (Courtesy of the Bostonian Society)

1778

John Hancock hosts a dinner at his home at today's **29 Beacon Street** on Beacon Hill for French Count Charles Hector d'Estaing and his officers. The purpose of the dinner is to thank the French for their support of the new Colonial government. When the milk runs out during the meal, Hancock's wife, Dorothy, dispatches servants to milk all of the cows on Boston Common and tells them to send anyone who complains to her.

1779

May 1. The General Court orders the estates of Loyalists to be confiscated for the benefit of the government.

1780

May 19. The "Dark Day" occurs. The sun is mysteriously obscured, causing great alarm in the town. It later turns out that the darkness was caused by smoke from a forest fire in Maine.

June 15. The **Massachusetts Constitution** is ratified at a meeting at the Brattle Square Church on the site of today's **City Hall Plaza**. The oldest written constitution in continued use in the world, much of it is written by John Adams, including the phrase "to the end it may be a government of laws and not of men."
September 4. **John Hancock** is elected the first governor of Massachusetts. He is re-elected every year through 1793, except for 1785–1787 when James Bowdoin holds the office.

The **Warren Tavern** opens at today's **2 Pleasant Street** in Charlestown. The oldest continuously operated tavern in the U.S., the building is enlarged in 1786 and renovated in 1972, and continues in business today.

1781

October 25. In ***Commonwealth v. Jennison***, a Massachusetts court frees slave Quock Walker of Barre from his master, Nathaniel Jennison. The Massachusetts Supreme Judicial Court upholds the decision in 1783, finding that by declaring "all men are born free and equal," the Massachusetts constitution effectively abolished slavery in the commonwealth.

October 26. An extra edition of the **Boston Gazette** announces Washington's victory over Cornwallis at Yorktown on October 17. The victory is celebrated with a huge bonfire on **Boston Common** on November 2.

1782

September 19. **Harvard Medical School** is founded. The third in the U.S., its creation was spurred by Dr. John Warren. Classes begin the following year in Cambridge. The school moves to Boston in 1810 and to its current location on **Longwood Avenue** in the Fenway in 1906.

1783

May 23. **James Otis** is killed by a bolt of lightning while standing in the doorway of his home in Andover. A few years earlier, Otis had written to his sister: "I hope when God Almighty, in his righteous Providence, shall take me out of time into eternity, that it will be by a flash of lightning." Otis is buried in the Granary Burying Ground.

July 4. Boston becomes the first town to designate and celebrate Independence Day as an official holiday. Dr. John Warren, brother of Joseph, the "martyr of Bunker Hill," delivers the first annual July 4 oration at **Faneuil Hall**.

1784

March 17. The Massachusetts legislature votes to hang the "**Sacred Cod**" in the chambers of the House of Representatives in the Old State House. "A memorial to the importance of cod fishing to the welfare of the Commonwealth," the 4' x 11' pine sculpture is moved to the chambers of the House of Representatives in the new Massachusetts State House on March 7, 1895.

In an article entitled "**Sentiments on Libertinism**" in the *Boston Magazine*, the author declares it unfair that a single act of infidelity should "forever deprive women of all that renders life valuable" while "the base betrayer (the man) is suffered to triumph in the success of his unmanly arts, and to pass unpunished even by a frown."

July 5. The **Manufactory House** (later Massachusetts Bank) opens on today's **Hamilton Place**. The second commercial bank in the Colonies (after the Bank of North America in Philadelphia), it merges with the First National Bank of Boston in 1903, and its successor is acquired by Bank of America in 2004.

1785

July 2. **Samuel Adams** complains about Boston residents in a letter to **John Adams** in France. There are, he writes, "too many citizens . . . who are imitating the Britons in every idle Amusement & expensive Foppery which it is in their power to invent for the Destruction of a young Country."

1786

June 17. The **Charles River Bridge** opens on **North Washington Street**, connecting the North End to Charlestown. The event attracts 20,000 people—more than the population of the entire town. A "Madam Healy" pays $500 to be the first person to cross the bridge and is driven over in a carriage drawn by four white horses. The current **Gilmore Bridge**, named for a former state representative from Charlestown, opens in 1899.

The Declaration of Independence is hailed in Boston (copyright 1943 by the New England Mutual Life Insurance Company, now MetLife).
(Courtesy of the Bostonian Society)

1787

Charles Bulfinch returns to Boston from a yearlong "Grand Tour of Europe"—and, in his words, goes about "pursuing no business but giving gratuitous advice in architecture." "Much as one might like to say something new about Bulfinch here," architectural historian Douglass Shand-Tucci later writes, "the old and venerable idea that he virtually created Boston architecturally is more or less true."

A correspondent for Philadelphia's **Columbian Magazine** writes of Boston: "Arts and sciences seem to have made greater progress here, than in any part of America."

October 17. **Prince Hall** and 13 other "freemen" of Boston petition the Massachusetts legislature to establish schools for African-American children, arguing that "our children . . . now receive no benefit from the free schools in the town of Boston, which we think is a great grievance." the petition is unsuccessful and African-American residents start their own school in the home of Hall's son, Primus, at the corner of **West Cedar** and **Revere Streets** on Beacon Hill in 1798.

November 18. King's Chapel at **58 Tremont Street** becomes the first **English Unitarian** church in Boston when James Freeman is ordained as the first American clergyman to call himself a Unitarian. Henry Adams later writes, "Nothing quieted doubt so completely as the mental calm of the Unitarian clergy. Doubts were a waste of thought."

Frog Pond, Boston Common, as it appears today. (Photograph by Richard Tourangeau)

1788

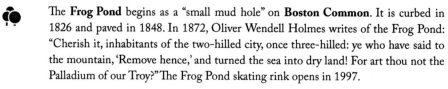

The **Frog Pond** begins as a "small mud hole" on **Boston Common**. It is curbed in 1826 and paved in 1848. In 1872, Oliver Wendell Holmes writes of the Frog Pond: "Cherish it, inhabitants of the two-hilled city, once three-hilled: ye who have said to the mountain, 'Remove hence,' and turned the sea into dry land! For art thou not the Palladium of our Troy?" The Frog Pond skating rink opens in 1997.

Brissot de Warville writes of Boston women: "They unite simplicity of morals with that French politeness and delicacy of manners which render virtue more amiable. The young women here enjoy the liberty they do in England,—that they did in Geneva when morals were there, and the Republic existed; and they do not abuse it."

November 2. The first public **Catholic Mass** in Boston takes place in the Church of the Holy Cross at today's **20 School Street**. It is celebrated by l'Abbe de la Poterie, a former chaplain for the French navy, in a building had been a French Huguenot chapel.

1789

The Power of Sympathy is published. Considered the first novel published in America, it is a thinly disguised story of a scandal in the family of **Sarah Wentworth Morton**, who lives at today's **28 State Street** and is at first thought to be the author. In fact, the book was written by her neighbor, **William Hill Brown**.

October 24. **George Washington** makes his first presidential visit to Boston and is greeted by huge crowds and a procession to the Old State House. But he is *not* greeted by Governor **John Hancock**, who thinks that the protocol should be for the president to call on him. Hancock relents two days later, however, when—carried on a litter and pleading an attack of gout—he visits Washington at the Ingersoll Inn at today's **10 Tremont Street**. The gesture is seen as symbolizing the acceptance of federal authority over that of individual states.

1790

According to the first U.S. Census Bureau, Boston's population is 18,320. It is the third largest town in the country after New York and Philadelphia.

(ca.) The **Deacon John Larkin House** is built at **55 Main Street** in Charlestown. The owner is famous for lending his horse, *Brown Beauty*, to Paul Revere on April 18, 1775—and never getting it back.

August 9. The *Columbia* returns to Boston. The first American ship to circumnavigate the globe, its voyage is credited with opening up a new triangular trade route for Boston merchants—one in which manufactured goods are exchanged in the Pacific Northwest for furs, which are then exchanged in China for tea, textiles, and porcelain.

1791

January 24. The **Massachusetts Historical Society** is founded. The oldest organization of its kind in the country, its headquarters are located initially in the attic of Faneuil Hall. The organization moves to its current location at **1154 Boylston Street** in 1899.

April 6. **John Stewart** is hanged on **Boston Common** for several robberies committed in homes on Pearl Street. It is reported that the thief's "plunder" was found in a tomb on Copp's Hill and he was "traced and caught one stormy night."

1792

August 10. The **New Exhibition Room** opens in a converted stable on today's **Hawley Street**. The first theater in Boston, the opening night performance is more a variety show than a play. When Sheridan's *A School for Scandal* opens on December 3, the performance is stopped and the theater manager is arrested for violating the laws against theatrical exhibitions. Public protest leads to the arrest being waived and the performances continue.

1793

January 21. The **Franklin Medals** are first distributed to the top (male) scholars in Boston's schools. An equal number of "**City Medals**" are given to girls beginning in 1821.

November 23. The **West Boston Bridge** opens at **Cambridge Street**, connecting Boston to Cambridge. It is replaced by the current **Longfellow Bridge**, sometimes called the "Salt and Pepper Bridge" for its distinctive towers, in 1906.

1794

February 3. The **Boston Theatre** opens at today's **1 Federal Street**. Designed by

Charles Bulfinch, it is the first true theater in Boston. Performers would include Edwin Forrest, Edmund Kean, and William Charles Macready. The building burns down in 1798 and, rebuilt, is for the next 30 years, Boston's premier—and only—theater. It is replaced by a second Boston Theatre in 1854.

French chef Jean Baptiste Gilbert Playpat opens **Julien's Restorator** at the corner of Milk and Congress Streets. Until now, establishments that sold meals had been called "cook-houses," but Julien's popularizes the use of the French word *restaurant*.

1795

February 27. The **Jamaica-Pond Aqueduct Company** is incorporated. Boston's first public water service, it purchases the water rights to **Jamaica Pond** and builds a 45-mile system of wooden pipes to bring water into Boston and Roxbury.

The **Bell-in-Hand Tavern** opens at today's **Exchange** and **State Streets**. The oldest continuously operated tavern in the original town of Boston, it moves to Pi Alley in 1853, a location Rufus Choate later describes as "ignominious but convenient." The tavern is today located at **45 Union Street** in Dock Square.

1796

The **Boston Dispensary** is established in Bartlett's apothecary shop on Cornhill. The first permanent medical institution in New England and third in the U.S., it moves to the South Cove in 1856 and subsequently merges with the Boston Floating Hospital and Pratt Diagnostic Clinic to form the New England Medical Center in 1965.

Gilbert Stuart paints the unfinished portraits *George Washington* and *Martha Washington (Martha Dandridge Custis)*. The paintings are acquired by the Boston Athenaeum in 1831 and are now owned jointly by the Museum of Fine Arts and the Smithsonian Institution's National Portrait Gallery.

1797

October 21. The USS *Constitution* (**"Old Ironsides"**) is launched from Edmund Hart's shipyard on the site of today's **U.S. Coast Guard Base** in the North End. The oldest commissioned ship in the U.S. Navy, the ship wins all 42 of its battles—including one over the HMS *Guerriere* in 1812 in which a sailor reportedly exclaims: "Huzza! Her sides are made of iron!" The U.S. Navy decommissions and considers scrapping the frigate in 1830, but a public outcry saves the ship and it is returned to Boston in 1897. The USS *Constitution* Museum is subsequently established in the **Charlestown Navy Yard,** where the ship is birthed today.

1798

January 11. The **Massachusetts State House** opens at today's **24 Beacon Street**. Designed by Charles Bulfinch, the red bricks are painted over in 1825 and then restored in 1928. The dome, originally covered in whitewashed wooden shingles, is sheathed in copper by Paul Revere & Son in 1802, covered in gold leaf in 1874, and painted gray to protect it from being a bombing target during World War II. A yellow

The State House and Beacon Hill between Hancock and Temple Streets. Lithograph after a drawing by J.R. Smith, 1811–1812. (Courtesy of the Bostonian Society)

brick addition to the rear is built in 1856 and 1895 and the white marble wings in 1917. They prompt Walter Muir Whitehill to describe the building as "a very odd fowl, indeed—with a golden topknot, a red breast, white wings, and a yellow tail."

1799

February 13. The **Boston Board of Health** is established. The first in the U.S., its duties are "to examine into all Nuisances & other causes injurious to the Health of the Inhabitants . . . and order such Nuisances to be removed." Paul Revere is the first president.

1800

By this date, the **Port of Boston** surpasses Philadelphia in both coastal and foreign trade and becomes second only to New York in total tonnage.

June 17. The **Charlestown Navy Yard** is created by order of the Massachusetts legislature. It is used primarily for storage, then for shipbuilding during the War of 1812 and the Civil War, then for repairing and converting ships belonging to the U.S. Navy. During World War II, 50,000 workers are employed in the yard—40% of them women. The federal government closes the yard and part of it is included in the Boston National Historic Park, which is established in 1974.

Grove Hall is built as a country house for Thomas Kilby Jones at the corner of **Blue Hill Avenue** and **Warren Street** in Roxbury. It later becomes a summer hotel, a sanitarium, a hospital, and then an orphanage. The complex of buildings is destroyed by a fire in July 1898.

1801

March. Charles Bulfinch's street plan for today's **South End** is adopted. The plan calls for English-style residential streets surrounding small parks. A plan by E.S. Chesborough and William Parrott is later added that calls for the streets to be bisected by French-style boulevards.

1802

The second **Harrison Gray Otis House** is completed at **85 Mount Vernon Street**. Designed by Charles Bulfinch, it is one of the only freestanding mansions on Beacon Hill. The building was used as the fictional residence of the hero in the 1968 movie *The Thomas Crown Affair* and today serves as the headquarters of the Colonial Society. **Pinebank** is built as a summer house for China Trade merchant James Perkins on the shore of **Jamaica Pond**. The original mansion is destroyed by fire and replaced. The second one is also destroyed by fire and replaced, with the third Pinebank completed in 1870. Acquired by the city in 1892, it serves as headquarters of the Parks Department, then as home to the Children's Museum and the Pinebank Center for the Arts. Damaged by another fire in 1978, the building is demolished in 2007.

Amos Upham opens a store in a former Federal-style house at the corner of **Dudley**, **Stoughton**, and **Boston Streets** in Dorchester, later called **Uphams Corner**. That building is replaced by a commercial building in 1884.

1803

The **Mount Vernon Proprietors** begin the developing Beacon Hill as a residential neighborhood by cutting down the top of what had been called Mount Vernon. The area had formerly been a "red light district," which prompts one of the developers to

India and Central Wharves, with the Norris and Baxter dining saloon in the foreground, 1857.
(Courtesy of the Bostonian Society)

write to another: "We are contracting to pull down . . . Mt. Whoredom. If you should not in the future resort to it with the same pleasure, you may possibly with more profit."

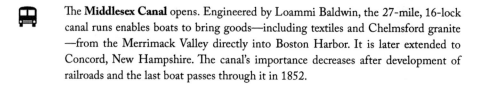

The **Middlesex Canal** opens. Engineered by Loammi Baldwin, the 27-mile, 16-lock canal runs enables boats to bring goods—including textiles and Chelmsford granite —from the Merrimack Valley directly into Boston Harbor. It is later extended to Concord, New Hampshire. The canal's importance decreases after development of railroads and the last boat passes through it in 1852.

September 29. The **Church of the Holy Cross** is dedicated at today's **214 Devonshire Street**. The first Catholic church built in Boston, it was built from plans donated by Charles Bulfinch with the support of a number of distinguished Protestants. The church becomes the Cathedral of the Holy Cross in 1808 and moves to its current location in the South End in 1875.*

1804

January 1. The **China Trade** begins in earnest, when **John Perkins Cushing**, the 16-year-old nephew of **Thomas Handasyd Perkins**, arrives at Canton and quickly establishes a close relationship with the Chinese merchant Houqua, later described as the richest man in the world. The Perkins company trades furs, ginseng, cash, cotton—and later opium—for Chinese tea, silks, and porcelain. So-called "Boston men" dominate the China Trade until it declines in the 1830s.

March 6. **South Boston** is annexed to Boston. The area is slow to attract residents, however, and architectural historian Walter Kilham later writes that the failure of fashionable Bostonians to flock to "the breezy hills of South Boston with their splendid marine views is one of the unsolved questions in Boston's history."

The **Thomas Amory** house is completed at **9 Park Street**. Designed by Charles Bulfinch for a wealthy merchant, it is the largest house in Boston at the time and is later divided into a number of residences. Harvard historian George Ticknor later occupies the southern half and there compiles the largest private library in the U.S. at the time. Today, the bottom floor is occupied by the restaurant No. 9 Park.

1805

Gilbert Stuart returns to Boston, where he lives until his death 20 years later. Born in Rhode Island, he is the premier portrait painter of the time. "In England my efforts were compared to those of Van Dyck, Titian and other greater painters," he tells a friend. "But here! They compare them to the works of the Almighty!" Yet Stuart also calls Boston a "cage" and complains that "a grocer will make more by buying a cargo of molasses in a day than my labor can make in a year." He dies in poverty in 1828 and is buried in an unmarked grave in the **Central Burying Ground**.

1806

February 13. The *Favorite* sails from Tudor Wharf in Charlestown packed with 130 tons of ice bound for the West Indies. Businessman **Frederic Tudor**'s venture is first derided in Boston newspapers as a "slippery one" in which "his assets will perceptibly melt away." But by the 1830s, Tudor is dubbed the "Ice King" and ships 50,000 tons of ice annually to destinations as far away as Calcutta and Rio de Janeiro. The industry does "melt away," however, after the invention of ice-making machinery in the 1860s.

December 6. The **African Meeting House** (originally First African Baptist Church) is dedicated at today's **8 Smith Court** on Beacon Hill. The congregation, which had been formed the year before and met first in Faneuil Hall, is the oldest African-American Baptist congregation in New England and the first outside the South. The building was constructed almost exclusively by African-American labor. The congregation later moves to the South End and merges with two others to form the Peoples Baptist Church. The building is sold to the Anshei Libovitz congregation of Hasidic Jews in 1898, and then purchased, restored, and reopened by the Museum of Afro-American History in 1988.

1807

August 5. The **Charles Street Meeting House** (originally Third Baptist Church) opens at today's **111–125 Charles Street**. Designed by Asher Benjamin, speakers from its pulpit would include Frederick Douglass, William Lloyd Garrison, Wendell Phillips, Harriet Tubman, and Sojourner Truth. The building is sold to the Charles Street A.M.E. Church in 1876 and is today used for commercial and residential purposes.

December. The **Embargo Act of 1807** goes into effect. Since more than one-third of

The African Meeting House at Smith Court at Joy Street. Photograph by Josiah J. Hawes, ca. 1860. (Courtesy of the Bostonian Society)

the new nation's British imports pass through the Port of Boston, the law particularly hurts the town. Some Boston merchants petition the president to end the embargo, others ignore the law; some talk of secession.

1808

 April 18. **Jean-Louis Lefebvre de Cheverus** is appointed the first Catholic bishop of Boston. The Boston Catholic archdiocese is established in October 1808. A scholar and a very diplomatic man, Cheverus later writes to John Carroll of Baltimore: "Papists are only tolerated. As long as our ministers behave, we will be tolerated. Let us expect no more than that."

1809

 January 19. **Edgar Allan Poe** is born in a boardinghouse at today's **62 Charles Street South**, a building that was torn down in 1959 is now the site of a parking lot. The son of actors, Poe lives in Boston for only a few months and comes to have less than positive feelings toward his hometown. After the *Boston Transcript* describes his reading of "The Raven" at the Odeon Theatre at **1 Federal Street** in 1845 as a "singularly didactic excordium," Poe writes: "We like Boston. We were born there—and perhaps it is just as well not to mention that we are heartily ashamed of the fact."

 The **Exchange Coffee House** opens at today's **21 Congress Street**. Designed by Asher Benjamin and built by Andrew Dexter, it is the first and most luxurious hotel in the U.S. Destroyed by a fire in 1818, it is subsequently rebuilt at a smaller scale.

1810

 January 10. **Park Street Church** is dedicated at today's **1 Park Street**. Designed by Peter Banner, it is the first Trinitarian-Congregationalist church in Boston. The church

is later called "Brimstone Corner"—owing either to the gunpowder stored in the basement during the War of 1812 or the fiery sermons preached there by ministers like the Rev. Lyman Beecher.

1811

February 25. **Massachusetts General Hospital** is chartered. The third general hospital in the U.S. (after those in Philadelphia and New York), its creation was sparked by Drs. James Jackson and John Collins Warren, who wrote a letter advocating construction of a hospital for "lunatics and other sick persons. . . one which would afford relief and comfort to thousands of the sick and miserable." A psychiatric hospital (later McLean Hospital) opens in 1816 and the general hospital itself in 1821.

1812

March 6. A map drawn by editor Nathan Hale of the newly redrawn Essex County state senate district which had been approved by Gov. Elbridge Gerry is published in the *Weekly Messenger* newspaper. A few days later, Joseph Cogswell shows the map to those attending a party at today's **52 Summer Street**. After one guest, painter Elkanah Tisdale, adds wings to the drawing, another notes that the shape looks like a salamander. That prompts a third, identified as "Mr. Alsop" to quip that it should be called a **"Gerrymander."** The term is used ever after to describe oddly-shaped electoral districts.

June 24. News that the **War of 1812** has been declared reaches Boston. Dorchester Heights is fortified against attack and the British blockade Boston Harbor. To identify true Bostonians from spies, guards ask soldiers and sailors: "What flies over Faneuil Hall?" The correct answer: "A grasshopper."

1813

June 1. The British frigate *Shannon* defeats the U.S. frigate *Chesapeake* off **Boston Light**. The American vessel is captured despite the order issued to the crew by its soon-to-die captain, James Lawrence: "Don't give up the ship."

Francis Cabot Lowell opens a textile mill on a dam across the Charles River in Waltham. The first complete textile factory in the world, it is credited with beginning the Industrial Revolution in America. Lowell had previously toured mills in England and Scotland and memorized their design. Returning to Boston, he worked with mechanic **Paul Moody** to replicate what he had seen.

1814

December 15. The **Hartford Convention** opens, attended by delegates from the various New England states and including representatives from Boston. Those in attendance are so opposed to the current war with Great Britain that they discuss secession. But the Treaty of Ghent is signed, ending the war, before the convention is adjourned.

1815

April 20. The **Handel and Haydn Society** is organized. It is the oldest oratorio society in the country. Its first concert is a performance of selections from Haydn's *Creation* and from Handel's *The Messiah* at King's Chapel at 58 Tremont Street on December 25.

May. The first issue of the ***North American Review*** appears. Founded by William Tudor and others, it is the premier magazine in the U.S. for many years, although W. S. Tryon later calls it "the oldest existing magazine in America, the most scholarly, the most honored, and the most unreadable."

1816

June 8. Snow falls in Boston during what is called the "Year without a Summer," in which frost is reported in every month.

October. The first annual **Brighton Fair and Cattle Show** is held at today's **54 Dighton Street** in Brighton. Sponsored by the Massachusetts Society for Promoting Agriculture, it continues until 1835.

1817

December 25. After a dispute in a card game, Lt. **Robert Massie** is killed in a duel by Lt. Gustavus Drane at **Fort Independence** on **Castle Island** in South Boston. Legend has it that Massie's friends avenge his death by getting Drane drunk, placing him in chains, and walling him up inside a dungeon of the fort—and that the tale later inspires **Edgar Allan Poe**, who is stationed at **Fort Independence** in 1827, to write the short story entitled "The Cask of Amontillado." In fact, Drane was court-martialed for his actions and acquitted, and he died in Philadelphia in 1846.

1818 (ca.)

Purple Windows are installed in homes on Beacon Hill when a shipment of glass from England arrives that has been discolored to a purple hue by a transformation of manganese oxide. The glass becomes a prized adornment and today can be seen in the windows of homes at **39, 40, 63** and **63 Beacon Street** and **29A** and **70B Walnut Street**.

1819

In a letter by William Tudor in the *North American Review*, Boston is first described as "**The Athens of America**." "This town is perhaps the most perfect and certainly the best-regulated democracy that ever existed," Tudor writes. "There is something so imposing in the immortal fame of Athens, that the very name makes everything modern shrink from comparison; but since the days of that glorious city I know of none that has approached so near in some points, distant as it may still be from that illustrious model."

August 16. Two sentries report sighting a sea serpent swim past **Castle Island**. Their superior, Col. Harris, verifies the sighting, as well as resident James Prince, who later describes the creature thus: "His head appeared about three feet out of the water; I counted thirteen bunches on his back—my family thought there were fifteen—he passed three times at a moderate rate across the bay. . . I had seven distinct views of

Looking west from the cupola of the State House toward Back Bay and the Mill Dam, 1863. (Courtesy of the Bostonian Society)

him from the long beach so called, and at some of them the animal was not more than a hundred yards distance."

1820

April 26. The **Siloam Lodge No. 2 of Odd Fellows** is organized. The second Odd Fellows lodge in the America, it is the second fraternal organization in Boston after the Masons.

1821

February 12. **Edmund Kean** makes his Boston debut at the Boston Theatre at today's **1 Federal Street**, appearing in a repertory of works by Shakespeare. After one performance, Kean receives what is thought to be the first curtain call in American theater history. But before another, he refuses to go on stage because the audience is so small. Boston theatergoers remember the slight, and when he returns in 1825 he is booed off the stage and forced to flee in disguise back to New York.

May. **English High School** opens on **Derne Street** on Beacon Hill. The first free public high school in the U.S., it is intended for "furnishing young men of the City who are not intended for a collegiate course of study . . . with the means of completing a good English education." Graduates would include Minister Louis Farrakhan, J.P. Morgan, Leonard Nimoy, and Louis Sullivan. The school moves several times and is today located at **144 McBride Street** in Jamaica Plain.

July 2. The **Mill Dam** is completed from Charles Street to Sewall's Point in Brookline (today's Kenmore Square) along today's **Beacon Street** in the Back Bay. It is built by the Boston and Roxbury Mill Dam Corporation, which promised it would power numerous gristmills and lower the price of bread in town. Few of the mills are ever

built, however, and the dam instead turns the Back Bay into a stagnant water pool of mudflats choked with debris and sewage with frogs, according to one visitor, "a foot high, and some as long as a child one year old."

1822

March 4. After years of unsuccessful attempts, Boston voters finally agree—by a margin of 2,797 to 1,881—to incorporate as a city. **John Phillips** is elected the first mayor of Boston on April 16.

May 1. The new city charter goes into effect. It calls for replacing the Town Meeting and Selectmen with a Mayor, an eight-member Board of Aldermen elected at-large, and a 48-member Common Council with four representatives elected from each ward.

1823

April 14. **Josiah Quincy** is elected the second mayor of Boston. A former congressman, state senator, speaker of the Massachusetts House, and judge, Quincy would be re-elected to five more one-year terms and later called the "great mayor." Known for rising before dawn every day to survey the city on horseback, Quincy reorganizes executive departments, leads police raids, establishes a regular sanitation and street-cleaning system, initiates the first municipal sewer system in the U.S., and completes the city's first successful urban renewal project in 1826.*

1824

Merchant **Andrew Eliot Belknap** campaigns against development of **Boston Common**. In an editorial he writes: "It is attempted to make us believe that this ornament of our city is reserved for the enjoyment of the rich alone, and that there exists amongst us a mean spirit of jealousy between the poor and the opulent. This is base calumny.. . . The common is emphatically called the poor man's inheritance; and it is, for all may enjoy it."

August 24. **Marquis de Lafayette** visits Boston. Ceremonies and receptions are held in his honor all over town, and during his stay a number of streets, squares, and parks are named in his honor, including **La Grange Street**, which is named after his summer residence. During his visit, Lafayette tells Boston Mayor Josiah Quincy: "You cannot understand the difference between a crowd in Europe and here in Boston; why, I should imagine the people of your city were a picked population out of the whole human race."

1825

The **Brattle Book Shop** is opened by Thomas M. Burnham, originally in the basement of Old South Meeting House at today's **310 Washington Street**. The oldest antiquarian bookstore in continuous operation in the U.S., it moves soon after to Cornhill. George Gloss purchases the store in 1949 and it moves several times thereafter. The store is operated today by Gloss's son, Ken, and it moves to its current location at **9 West Street** in 1969.

July 22. The **"Beehive Riots"** begin when a mob engages in the first of a weeklong series of raids on brothels in the North End. The riots lead to destruction of property and force women known euphemistically as "the nymphs of Ann Street" to flee. Ann Street is renamed **North Street** in 1854.

October. The **Erie Canal** is completed, helping New York City surpass Boston as the major port in the U.S. In an attempt to remain competitive, the Massachusetts legislature had appointed a commission to "ascertain the practicability of making a canal from Boston Harbor to Connecticut River" and "of extending the same to some point on the Hudson River . . . in the vicinity of the junction of the Erie Canal." According to historian Samuel Eliot Morison, however, "Massachusetts wisely accepted the veto of her topography" and the idea was not pursued any further.

1826

The **Union Oyster House** opens at today's **41 Union Street**. Originally Atwood and Bacon Oyster House, it is now the oldest continuously operated restaurant in the U.S. Its patrons include Daniel Webster, who was known for eating six plates of oysters at a sitting and washing them down with as many brandy-and-waters. The restaurant also claims to be the first in the country to offer wooden toothpicks in 1869.

A **high school for girls** opens on **Derne Street** on Beacon Hill. The first in the U.S., the school is "kept open eighteen or nineteen months, during which time not one pupil voluntarily quitted it, nor would as long as they could be allowed to stay, except in case of marriage." The cost per student is estimated at $11 per year. It is closed two years later, however, by Boston Mayor Josiah Quincy, who declares: "No city could stand the expense."

August 26. **Quincy Market** opens. Designed by Alexander Parris, it is considered the first urban renewal project in the Colonies and is built on land created by filling in the Town Dock area. The cost of its construction is quickly repaid by the rents charged to merchants, prompting Boston Mayor Josiah Quincy to boast that it was "was accomplished in the centre of a populous city, not only without any tax, debt or burden upon its pecuniary resources but with large permanent additions to its real and productive property." The market is renovated and reopens in 1976.*

1827

Durgin-Park restaurant opens at today's **340 Faneuil Hall Marketplace**. Originally a small eating place catering to market and dockworkers, it is later described by Lucius Beebe as "not a restaurant (but) a dining room in the old New England manner" that contains waitresses "with notions of their own as to what patrons ought to eat and ideas of table service that would make the hair of a French waiter captain stand up on his head." The restaurant continues to operate and the waitresses continue to have those ideas and notions today.

Papanti's Dance Studio is opened by Count Lorenzo Papanti of Tuscany. The studio proves extremely popular with members of Boston's social elite. When Papanti builds a new studio at today's **17 Tremont Street**, it includes the first ballroom in the country with a dance floor constructed on springs—in order to better accommodate one of his

A view of Faneuil Hall Marketplace from the east. Lithograph by John Andrews. (Courtesy of the Bostonian Society)

most generous—and generously proportioned—students Mrs. Harrison Gray Otis. The studio continues to operate until 1899.

July 23. **Jarvis Braman's Bath House** opens at the foot of **Chestnut Street** on Beacon Hill. It includes the first swimming pool in the U.S., a 150-foot-square saltwater pool, where the first swimming classes are held. John Quincy Adams and John James Audubon are among the first students.

1828

Girls are finally allowed to attend Boston's public grammar schools for the entire school year. They are also allowed to continue in school until 16 years of age, while boys are required to leave at 14.

December 15. **Josiah Quincy** fails to win re-election for a seventh consecutive one-year term. Some historians attribute his loss to firefighters angry at Quincy's refusal to appoint their candidate chief engineer others to his closing of the high school for girls. The *Boston Patriot* newspaper later credits the "laboring class vote" for his defeat and criticizes Quincy for his "haughty anti-republican manners." He goes on to become president of Harvard College.

1829

January 1. The first illuminating gas streetlight in Boston is installed at Dock Square. Gas streetlights begin to replace oil lamps across the city and by 1834 there are 10,000 of them. The last gaslights are removed in 1958, but they are later reintroduced in some historic neighborhoods.

March 17. The **Massachusetts Horticultural Society** is founded. The second oldest group of its kind in the U.S. after one in Pennsylvania, it moves to its current

location, Horticultural Hall at **300 Massachusetts Avenue,** in 1901. The organization first sponsors its annual Spring Flower Show in 1871.

The **Old Corner Bookstore** opens at today's **3 School Street.** Later nicknamed "Parnassus Corner" after the Greek mountain home of the Muses, it becomes the center of the town's intellectual life and a meeting place for writers including Alcott, Emerson, Fuller, Hawthorne, Holmes, Howe, Longfellow, Stowe, Thoreau, and Whittier. William D. Ticknor and John Allen take over the operation in 1832. James Fields becomes Ticknor's partner in 1854. Threatened with demolition, the building is purchased and preserved by Historic Boston Inc. in 1960.

September 5. The first issue of *The Pilot* appears. The first Catholic newspaper in the U.S., it is founded by Bishop Fenwick, and later sold to private owners, but reacquired by the Catholic Archdiocese of Boston in 1908 and continues to publish today.

September. ***David Walker's Appeal . . . to the Coloured Citizens of the World, but In Particular, and Very Expressly, to Those of the United States of America*** is published. Written by the African-American proprietor of a Brattle Street clothing store, it calls on slaves to fight for their freedom. When the book is distributed in the South, some of the region's governors call for Walker's arrest. After receiving numerous threats, Walker is found dead on the street on June 28, 1830. Some believe he was poisoned, others that his death was caused by a seizure or tuberculosis.

October 16. **Tremont House** opens at today's **1 Beacon Street.** Designed by Isaiah Rogers, it is the most elegant and modern hotel in America at the time. Guests can rent single rooms (rather than "double up" with strangers as has been the practice until now) and each room comes with a key, washbowl, pitcher, free soap, and gaslights. Guests would include Charles Dickens, who writes that the hotel has more "galleries, colonnades, piazzas and passages than I can remember, or the reader would believe." The building is demolished in 1895.

1830
Boston's population is 61,392, double what it had been 20 years earlier. It is the fourth largest of any city in the U.S. after New York, Baltimore, and Philadelphia.

"It was a time," Lawrence Lader later wrote of the 1830s, "when almost every thinking Bostonian was convinced that the world could be remade at his doorstep. It was an age of unbounded confidence when Boston set out to re-create its own image of heaven on Beacon Hill."

July 24. The first issue of the ***Boston Evening Transcript*** appears. The city's first afternoon daily, it "reflected the atmosphere of old Boston." according to journalist Louis Lyons. One joke has it that a Back Bay butler once announced to his master: "Three reporters are at the door, sir, and a gentleman from the *Transcript.*" Located originally on Exchange Street, the newspaper moves to its own building at **324 Washington Street** in 1872. Its last issue appears on April 30, 1941.

The Liberator masthead. (Courtesy of the Bostonian Society)

1831

➹ *January 1.* The first issue of *The Liberator* appears. Published first from offices at today's **60 Congress Street**, the abolitionist weekly newspaper is founded by **William Lloyd Garrison** "to lift up the standard of emancipation in the eyes of the nation, within the sight of Bunker Hill, and in the birthplace of liberty." It is credited with helping to undermine the symbiotic relationship Charles Sumner later describes as between the "Lords of the Lash" (owners of cotton plantations in the South) and the "Lords of the Loom" (owners of textile factories in the North). The newspaper continues to publish until the Thirteenth Amendment, which prohibits slavery, goes into effect on December 18, 1865.

1832

➹ *January 6.* The **New England Anti-Slavery Society** is founded by **William Lloyd Garrison** and 11 other white men at a meeting at the African Meeting House at today's **8 Smith Court**. The first antislavery organization in the country, it becomes the most influential abolitionist organization in Boston. At the meeting, Garrison declares: "We have met to-night in this obscure school-house; our numbers are few and our influence limited; but, mary my prediction, Faneuil Hall shall ere long echo with the principles we have set forth. We shall shake the nation by their mighty power." The Boston Female Anti-Slavery Society is founded by **Lydia Maria Child** and **Maria Weston Chapman** on October 14.

✳ *August.* The **Perkins Institution for the Blind** opens in the home of its founder, Samuel Gridley Howe, at what was then **140 Pleasant Street**. The first school for the blind in the U.S., it has six students in the first class. Originally the New England Institution for the Education of the Blind, the school is renamed for Thomas Handasyd Perkins, who donates his home to the school at 17 Pearl Street in 1833. The school moves to South Boston in 1839 and to its current location in Watertown in 1912.

✳ *October 24.* The **Boston Lying-In Hospital** opens at **718 Washington Street**. Founded to care for "poor and deserving women during confinement," it moves several times before relocating to Longwood Avenue in 1923, merges with the Free Hospital for

Women to become Boston Hospital for Women in 1965, and becomes part of Brigham and Women's Hospital in 1981.

1833

April 19. The **East Boston Company** is incorporated by **William Hyslop Sumner** and others. The company subsequently begins filling in marshes and connecting Noddles, Hog, Bird, Governor's, and Apple Islands in Boston Harbor to create today's East Boston.

June 24. President **Andrew Jackson** receives an honorary degree from Harvard College. **Josiah Quincy Jr.**, whose father is the former mayor of Boston and current president of Harvard, attends the ceremony and later writes that while he expected Jackson to be "simply intolerable to the Brahmin caste of my native State," he finds him instead to be "a gentleman [with a] high sense of honor." Quincy's use of the term **"Brahmin"** pre-dates what is generally cited as the first use of the term by Oliver Wendell Holmes in his 1861 novel, *Elsie Venner*.

Title page of K. N.: Six Hours in a Convent; or, The Stolen Nuns! A Tale of Charlestown in 1834, a book about the fire at the Ursuline Convent. (Courtesy of the Bostonian Society)

1834

The **first waltz** is danced in Boston by **Mrs. Harrison Gray Otis** and **Lorenzo Papanti** at a party at the Otis mansion at today's **1 Somerset Street**. Respectability comes slowly for the waltz in Boston, however. According to Cleveland Amory, a father who dragged his daughter away from her partner later wrote to a friend: "I can only describe the position they were in as the very reverse of back-to-back." It would be exactly 100 years later that **Mrs. E. Sohier Welch** launches Boston's annual "waltz evenings," first at her home on Louisburg Square, then at the Hotel Somerset and Copley Plaza Hotel.

August 11. The **Ursuline Convent** is burned down by a mob of teamsters and brick-yard workers in an area of Charlestown that is today part of Somerville. The mob was not only aroused by anti-Catholic feelings but by rumors that one of the nuns was being held against her will. Neither police nor fire department officials attempted to intervene. Although the state legislature later deplores the crime, it refuses to reimburse the Catholic diocese for damages. The burned convent remains standing until the land is sold in 1875.

Bird's-eye view of Boston, drawn by J. Bachman. (Courtesy of the Bostonian Society)

1835

April 8. **Charlotte Cushman** makes her stage debut in a supporting role in *The Marriage of Figaro* at the Tremont Theatre at today's **82 Tremont Street**. Born at **25 Parmenter Street** in the North End and later a resident of Charlestown, Cushman becomes one of the greatest actresses of her era. Her last Boston appearance is at the Globe Theatre on May 15, 1875.

May 3. The **Abiel Smith School** is dedicated at today's **46 Joy Street**. The first public primary school for African-American children in the U.S., it is later boycotted by their parents, who prefer that their children attend integrated schools. The school closes after a state law prohibiting segregated public schools is passed in 1855.

October 21. **William Lloyd Garrison** is attacked by a mob—or, according to the *Boston Commercial Gazette*, "an assemblage of fifteen hundred or two thousand highly respectable gentlemen"—at the Boston Female Anti-Slavery Society at **46 Washington Street**. The mob chases and catches Garrison, ties a rope around his neck, and threatens to lynch him until he is rescued by Boston **Mayor Theodore Lyman Jr.** and city constables. The *Boston Transcript* later blames Garrison for the attack—because he "excited the people to such an abullition of their deeply exasperated feelings."

1836

September 19. The first meeting of the **Transcendentalist Club** takes place in the parsonage of George Ripley, pastor of the Thirteenth Congregational Church on **Purchase Street**. Originally called "The Club," or "Hedge's Club" after Frederic Henry Hedge, its original members also include Bronson Alcott, James Freeman Clarke, Ralph Waldo Emerson, Converse Francis, and George Putnam. Margaret Fuller and Elizabeth Peabody are subsequently invited to join soon after. William H. Channing later describes Transcendentalism as "an assertion of the inalienable integrity of man, of the immanence of divinity of instinct. On the somewhat stunted stock of Unitarianism . . . had been grafted German Idealism. . . and the result was a vague, yet exalting conception of the godlike nature of the human spirit." The club meets in the homes of various members and continues until 1840.

1837

James Allen's *The Life of a Highwayman* is published. The book is the autobiography of a man executed for robbery and is bound in leather made from the author's own skin. Two copies are printed. One is today in the possession of the **Boston Athenaeum**.

June 11. The **"Broad Street Riot"** breaks out when Irish mourners at a Catholic funeral clash with Protestant firefighters returning from a fire. Eventually, an estimated 15,000 people take part. Boston Mayor **Samuel A. Eliot** calls out the militia and personally leads the troops against the rioters, getting knocked down several times in the process. Order is finally restored several hours later.

August 31. **Ralph Waldo Emerson** delivers "**The American Scholar**" Phi Beta Kappa address at Harvard College. Later called by Oliver Wendell Holmes "our intellectual Declaration of Independence," the speech calls on Americans to stop imitating the "courtly muses of Europe" and declares that "our day of dependence, our long apprenticeship to the learning of other lands, draws to a close."

November 6. The **Boston Public Garden** is founded by **Horace Gray** and other amateur horticulturists at the intersection of today's **Beacon** and **Charles Streets**. The group proceeds to build a garden, greenhouse, and birdhouse on 24 acres of formerly marshy land. After Gray loses his fortune, the park falls into disrepair. The city reclaims the property and, following a plan by George Meacham, completes the park in the early 1860s. The lagoon bridge, designed by William G. Preston, opens in 1867 and the Swan Boats, designed and operated **Robert Paget**, in 1877. Paget's family still operates the boats today.

Little, Brown and Company is founded by Charles C. Little and James Brown. The oldest publishing company in the U.S., it publishes Louisa May Alcott's *Little Women*, Edward Everett Hale's *Man Without a Country*, and the poetry of Emily Dickinson. The company's headquarters is located for many years in the former Cabot mansion at **31 Beacon Street**. It moves to New York after being acquired by Warner Communications in 1989.

1838

February 21. **Angelina Grimké** becomes the first woman to testify before a legislative body in the U.S. when she delivers an antislavery petition signed by 20,000 women at the Massachusetts State House at **24 Beacon Street** on Beacon Hill. "I stand before you as a moral being," she declares, "and as a moral being I feel that I owe it to the suffering slave and to the deluded master, to my country and to the world, to do all that I can to overturn a system of complicated crimes built upon the broken hearts and prostrate bodies of my countrymen in chains and cemented by the blood, sweat and tears of my sisters in bonds." Angelina spoke only because her sister, Sarah, was sick.

The **Ropewalk Building** is completed at the **Charlestown Navy Yard**. Designed by Alexander Parris, the two-story granite building is one-quarter of a mile long and all of the rope used by the U.S. Navy is subsequently produced here. "Way back then," the *Boston Herald* later reports, "(rope was) as important as nuclear fission . . . and private industry was perhaps less reliable and less capable in those days." Rope production continues in the building until 1971.

1839

The **Tremont Temple** (originally First Baptist Free Church) is founded. The first integrated church in America, the congregation meets at various locations before building the first of its three church buildings at its current location at **88 Tremont Street**. Speakers in the church would include every U.S. president from Lincoln to Hoover, Eugene Debs, Charles Dickens, Frederick Douglass, William Lloyd Garrison, Rev. Billy Graham, Helen Keller, and Daniel Webster. It was after appearing at the Tremont Temple that Will Rogers commented: "I never met a man I didn't like."

1840

July 18. The *Britannia* arrives from Liverpool at the new Cunard Line terminal in East Boston providing the first passenger service to the U.S. by Samuel Cunard's North American Royal Mail Steam Packet Company. Although the line does not carry a significant number of immigrants until 1863, it spawns a number of lower-cost competitors, which leads to most of the 1.5 million Irish immigrants to the U.S. in the next few years coming though Boston. "The vast majority left their ships in East Boston," historian Oscar Handlin later writes, "without the slightest conception of how they would earn a livelihood and with only enough money to keep them fed and sheltered for a week or two."

July. The first issue of *The Dial* is published from offices at **121 Washington Street** in today's Government Center. Founded by Ralph Waldo Emerson and others, the quarterly journal is devoted to literature and religion and what comes to be known as Transcendentalism. Margaret Fuller is the first editor. The magazine continues to publish until 1843.

Elizabeth Palmer Peabody opens her Foreign Library and Bookshop in the parlor of her home at today's **15 West Street**. The shop becomes the unofficial headquarters for the "Transcendentalist Movement." Peabody's sister Sophia marries Nathaniel Hawthorne here in 1842, and her sister Mary marries Horace Mann here in 1843.

1841

April. The **Brook Farm Institute of Agriculture and Education** is founded by **Rev. George Ripley**, his wife, his sister, and a few friends on a 192-acre farm at today's **670 Baker Street in West Roxbury**. The goal of the experiment in communal living is "to approach more nearly the ideal of human society than any that has ever existed," and visitors come from as far away as Europe to view it. Although he declines to join, Ralph Waldo Emerson calls it a "French Revolution in miniature." Although he decides to leave after living there briefly, Nathaniel Hawthorne later reflects: "More

Bradford House,
Brook Farm,
West Roxbury. (Courtesy
of the Bostonian Society)

and more I feel we at Brook Farm struck upon what ought to be a truth. Posterity may dig it up and profit by it." His novel based on his experiences there, *The Blithedale Romance*, is published in 1852. Financial difficulties, an outbreak of smallpox, and a fire force the community to close in the fall of 1847.

1842

January 22. **Charles Dickens** arrives in Boston on board the *Britannia*. It is the first stop of a four-month tour of the U.S. and Canada. Reporters hire boats to meet Dickens's ship before it docks, and a huge crowd gathers to watch him come ashore and follows him to the Tremont House at today's **1 Beacon Street,** where he lodges. During his two-week stay, Dickens visits a number of the city's charitable institutions, including the Perkins Institution for the Blind and the House of Reformation for Juvenile Offenders. In *American Notes,* published a year later, Dickens writes: "The golden calf they worship at Boston is a pigmy compared with the giant effigies set up in other parts of that vast countinghouse which lies beyond the Atlantic, and the almighty dollar sinks into something comparatively insignificant amidst a whole Pantheon of better gods... Above all, I sincerely believe that the public institutions and charities of this capital of Massachusetts are as nearly perfect as the most considerate wisdom, benevolence, and humanity can make them. I never in my life was more affected."

The **Merchants Exchange Building** opens at today's **53 State Street**. Designed by Isaiah Rogers, it is later torn down to make way for the 11-story Stock Exchange Building, designed Peabody and Stearns, in 1891. That building is restored and joined to a new 40-story glass tower and renamed Exchange Place in 1984.

1843

June 17. The **Bunker Hill Monument** is dedicated in Charlestown. Designed by Solomon Willard, the 220-foot memorial is the first major monument to be built in the U.S. President John Tyler and 13 veterans of the battle attend the event, as does

The steamship Britannia, *surrounded by ice in Boston Harbor. Drawing by J.D. King.* (Courtesy of the Bostonian Society)

Daniel Webster, who declares in his speech that the monument shall cause "from every youthful breast, the ejaculation 'thank God, I—I also—AM AN AMERICAN.'"

July. **Margaret Fuller**'s essay "**Woman in the Nineteenth Century**" appears in *The Dial* magazine. In it, she argues that women do not want "money nor notoriety nor the badges of authority which men have appropriated to themselves . . . (but). . .the freedom, the religious, the intelligent freedom of the universe to use its means, to learn its secret as far as Nature has enabled them, with god alone for their guide and their judge." The essay is expanded and published as a book in 1845.

1844

April 21. **William Miller** and his followers in the Church of the Adventists don white robes and ascend to the roof of their wooden "tabernacle" called the Howard Athenaeum at what was then **34 Howard Street** in Scollay Square to await the end of the world. Nothing happens. Miller, a former a sheriff in Vermont, subsequently revises his doomsday prediction several times. When nothing happens after the final one on October 22, 1844, the congregation dissolves. The building is converted into a theater, which burns down and is rebuilt in 1846.*

Robert Gourlay's pamphlet, *General Plan for enlarging and improving the City of Boston*, is published. A visiting Scotsman and an insomniac who claims to have slept only two hours in the last five years, Gourlay's grandiose proposal includes building islands in the middle of the Charles River and the Back Bay. He does, however, correctly predict that the city's population will reach a half-million in 50 years, and he foresees the need to build underground subway lines throughout the city.

1845

The **Boston Associates** dominate business in Boston and Massachusetts. According to Robert F. Dalzell Jr., the group of about 80 men had interests in 31 textile companies

A view of the Water Celebration on Boston Common. Engraving by S. Rowse, 1848.
(Courtesy of the Bostonian Society)

and its members served as directors of banks that controlled over 40% of the city's authorized banking capital. According to Kurt Schriftgiesser, "They controlled the press and pulpit and politics of Massachusetts."

Donald McKay opens a shipyard on **Border Street** in East Boston. A freelance shipbuilder in New York, Maine, and Newburyport, McKay becomes the foremost builder of the majestic clipper ships. Naval historian Samuel Eliot Morison later describes McKay's *Flying Cloud* as ". . . our Rheims, the *Sovereign of the Seas* our Parthenon, the *Lightning* our Amiens." The *Flying Cloud* sets a record in sailing from New York to San Francisco in 89 days and eight hours in 1854.

October 27. **Maria Bickford** is killed in a rooming house on today's **Cedar Lane Way** on Beacon Hill. Her accused killer, **Albert Tirrell**, is a married man whose lawyer, Rufus Choate, employs a number of curious arguments in his client's defense—that the woman committed suicide; that if Tirrell did kill her, it was because she was leading him into sin; or that he killed her in his sleep. Tirrell ends up being acquitted of the charge in March 1846.

1846

Francis Tukey is appointed City Marshal. A Maine native and law school graduate, he presides over the growth of the Boston Police Department. Although his integrity was never questioned, his aggressive approach to law enforcement leads him to be described by the *Bunker Hill Aurora* as "a terror to evildoers and some who were not evildoers." A controversial figure, he is replaced in 1853 and leaves Boston for California.

October 16. The first successful public demonstration of ether takes place under what is later called the "**Ether Dome**" in the Bulfinch Building of Massachusetts General Hospital at **55 Fruit Street**. The anesthetic is administered by dentist **William T.G. Morton** to a 20-year-old patient who is having a tumor removed from his jaw. After the operation, surgeon John Collins Warren exclaims: "Gentlemen, this is no humbug!" Because of the controversy over whether Morton or others should be given credit for the discovery, no name appears on the statue known as "The Death of Pain" when it is dedicated in the Public Garden in 1868—prompting Oliver Wendell Holmes to suggest the name of the drug should be pronounced "Either."

August 31. The first issue of the **Boston Herald** appears. Originally the evening edition of the *Eagle*, it becomes the evening edition of the *Boston Traveler* in 1912, until the two merge to become the *Boston Herald Traveler* in 1967, then reverts back to being the *Boston Herald* in 1982. It is purchased by current owner Patrick Purcell in 1994 and is today one of the few independently owned major metropolitan newspapers in the country, located today at **70 Fargo Street** in South Boston.

October 5. The second **Howard Athenaeum** opens at **34 Howard Street** in Scollay Square. Designed by Isaiah Rogers, the granite, Gothic-style theater is the home first of opera and serious drama, then of vaudeville, and finally of burlesque. Among those who perform here are: Abbott; and Costello, Fred Allen, Jimmy Durante, W.C. Fields, Al Jolson, and Buster Keaton, then Ann Corio, Sally Keith, and Sally Rand. It is known for its advertisements, which proclaim "There is Always Something Doing at the **Old Howard**" and for offending the morals of proper Bostonians.

1847

The **Long Wharf Immigration Station** is established. Over 37,000 immigrants enter Boston during the year, most classified as "Irish labourers" fleeing the **Potato Famine** in their native country. Years earlier, Bishop Fenwick had advocated creating a colony for Irish immigrants in Maine, and over the next few years proposals would be made to establish such a colony in Iowa and in Canada. Edward Everett Hale later writes: "This transfer of immense bodies of people, from one climate, government, and state of society, to another wholly different is the most remarkable social phenomenon of our times."

May 20. The *American Signal*, a new, anti-Catholic and anti-immigrant newspaper asks: "Is this Boston? Or is it Dublin? Did our Pilgrim Fathers land on Plymouth Rock or was it in the Cove of Cork? Have we a right to the streets of the city where we were born or do they belong to is holiness, the Pope: Must we submit to be overrun by the paupers of English government? Shall our beloved country be forced by despots to become the POOR HOUSE OF THE WORLD?"

June 16. The **Custom House** opens at today's **3 McKinley Square**. Designed by Ammi Young in the Greek Revival style, it is built with Quincy granite quarried by Solomon Willard and is the most expensive government building of its time. A 32-story tower designed by Peabody & Stearns is added in 1915, making it the tallest in Boston until 1947.

1848

March 18. The **Boston Public Library** is incorporated. The first large, publicly sup-

Looking down Beacon Street from Bowdoin toward the Boston Athenaeum, ca. 1889. (Courtesy of the Bostonian Society)

ported, free municipal library in the U.S., it is also the first to allow borrowing of books and materials. The first library opens in the former Adams schoolhouse on **Mason Street** in 1854. A new library building opens at today's **106 Boylston Street**, and the current library in Copley Square opens in 1895.*

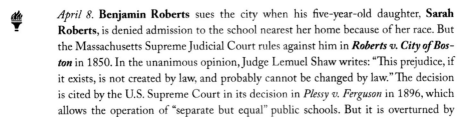

April 8. **Benjamin Roberts** sues the city when his five-year-old daughter, **Sarah Roberts,** is denied admission to the school nearest her home because of her race. But the Massachusetts Supreme Judicial Court rules against him in *Roberts v. City of Boston* in 1850. In the unanimous opinion, Judge Lemuel Shaw writes: "This prejudice, if it exists, is not created by law, and probably cannot be changed by law." The decision is cited by the U.S. Supreme Court in its decision in *Plessy v. Ferguson* in 1896, which allows the operation of "separate but equal" public schools. But it is overturned by *Brown v. Board of Education of Topeka* in 1954.

June 28. **Forest Hills Cemetery** opens at today's **95 Forest Hills Avenue** in Jamaica Plain. Designed by Gen. Henry A.S. Dearborn, it is the fourth "garden cemetery" and includes the first crematory in the U.S. Among those buried here are poets e.e. cummings and Anne Sexton, abolitionist William Lloyd Garrison, playwright Eugene O'Neill, and suffragist Lucy Stone. The 275-acre cemetery is also home to sculptures by Daniel Chester French, Martin Millmore, and others.

September 15. **Abraham Lincoln** speaks at a rally for presidential candidate Zachary Taylor at Washington Hall at today's **21 Bromfield Street**. He speaks at Richmond Hall at the corner of **Washington** and **Richmond Streets** in Dorchester the next day, and a few days later at a Free Soil Rally at Tremont Temple at **88 Tremont Street**.

October 25. A **Water Festival** attracts a crowd of 100,000 people to **Boston Common** to celebrate the opening of the aqueduct supplying Boston with water from Lake Cochituate. The crowd witnesses a plume of water rise 80 feet into the air from the Frog Pond, and the festivities that follow include speeches, cannon fire, and fireworks.

Immigrant arrival at Constitution Wharf, from Ballou's Pictorial.
(Courtesy of the Boston Public Library, Print Department)

October. A ship carrying a cargo of leather from California arrives in Boston and brings news of the **Gold Rush** that followed the discovery at Sutter's Mill. The *Sausalito* sails from Boston for California on December 2, carrying the first Bostonians bound for the gold fields.

1849

The **Back Bay** is described by the Boston Board of Health as "nothing less than a great cesspool into which is daily deposited all the filth of a large and constantly increasing population."

Lewis Hayden opens a custom and ready-made clothing business on **Cambridge Street**. A runaway slave from Kentucky, Hayden uses his profits and products to feed and cloth fugitive slaves he harbors at his home at **66 Phillips Street** on Beacon Hill, an important stop on the Underground Railroad. Hayden claims to keep two kegs of gunpowder in his basement, which he threatens to detonate if anyone attempts to search the house.

July. The **Boston Athenaeum** opens at **10½ Beacon Street**. The organization was founded in 1807. The building is designed by Edward Clarke Cabot in the Italianate style, with an addition by Henry Forbes Bigelow in 1914. It does not have a name but only the street address on the front door, according to Walter Muir Whitehill, because "of the general Boston assumption that anyone with serious business knows where things are; those who do not should inform themselves by other means than gaping at signs." Henry James later describes the building as "this honored haunt of all the most civilized," and David McCord as "a kind of Utopia for books [where] . . . the reader, the scholar, the browser, the borrower is king."

November 23. **Dr. George Parkman** disappears after leaving his home at **8 Walnut**

Street on Beacon Hill. In a massive investigation that follows, police reportedly round up "every Irishman with a dollar in his pocket" before arresting **Dr. John White Webster**, a professor at Harvard Medical School who had owed money to Parkman. Webster is subsequently convicted of murder after traces of Parkman's body are found in the drains of Harvard Medical School by the school janitor, Ephraim Littlefield. The trial captures national attention and prompts Harvard president Jared Sparks to declare: "Our Professors do not often commit murder." Webster is hanged at the Leverett Street Jail on August 30, 1850—within sight of the medical school where he had taught, which was built on land which had been donated by Parkman.

1850

Boston's population is 136,881, an increase of almost 50% in 10 years. There are 46,677 foreign-born residents—35,287 from Ireland.

January. In his inaugural address, recently re-elected Boston mayor **John P. Bigelow** declares: "Foreign paupers are rapidly accumulating on our hands. . . Numbers of helpless beings, including imbeciles, in both body and mind,—the aged, the blind, the paralytic, and the lunatic, have been landed from immigrant vessels, to become instantly, and permanently charge upon our public charities."

Elias Haskett Derby Jr. writes that, thanks to expanded railroad service, Boston businessmen can "reach their stores and offices in the morning, and at night sleep with their wives and children in the suburbs. No time is lost, for they read the morning and evening journals as they go and return."

Daniel Laing and **Isaac Snowden** of Boston and **Martin Delaney** of Pittsburgh become the first African-American students admitted to Harvard Medical School, then located on **North Grove Street** in the West End—but they are subsequently dismissed after protests by the other students convince the dean "that intermixing of the white and Black races. . . is distasteful to a large portion of the class and injurious to the interests of the school."
Harriot Kezia Hunt becomes the first woman to be accepted to Harvard Medical School—but is persuaded to withdraw, which the school announces: "Resolved, That no woman of true delicacy would be willing in the presence of men, to listen to the discussion of the subjects that necessarily come under the consideration of the student of medicine. Resolved, That we are not opposed to allowing woman her rights, but we do protest against her appearance where her presence is calculated to destroy our respect for the modesty and delicacy of her sex."

September 28. **Jenny Lind** makes her singing debut in Boston at Tremont Temple at today's **88 Tremont Street**. Seats are auctioned to the highest bidder (a common practice at the time) and Lind's popularity is dubbed "Lindamania" by the press. When she sings again at the Fitchburg Railroad Station in Boston on October 12, a thousand people pay a dollar each for standing-room tickets and a stampede occurs as the audience vies for the best seats.

1851

February 15. Runaway slave **Shadrach Minkins** is arrested at the Cornhill Coffee House, where he works as a waiter, and was located at today's **1 Beacon Street**. Brought to the Suffolk County Courthouse at **Court Square**, he is freed by a group of free African-Americans led by Lewis Hayden and eventually escapes to Montreal. *April 3.* Runaway slave **Thomas Sims** is also captured in Boston, but Marshal Tukey prevents efforts to free Sims by running a chain around the courthouse. Sims goes on trial and is found to be the property of James Potter of Georgia and ordered returned to his owner. Under heavy guard, Sims is marched past thousands of protesters to Long Wharf on April 19, put on a ship, and returned to Georgia.

September 17. A three-day **Railroad Jubilee** is held on **Boston Common** to celebrate the opening of the railroad line between Boston, the Great Lakes, and Canada. The event is attended by President Millard Fillmore and Secretary of State Daniel Webster, who had earlier commented: "The rich take the train because it is quicker, the poor because it is cheaper . . . In the history of human inventions there is hardly one so well calculated as that of railroads to equalize the condition of men . . . Men are thus brought together as neighbors and acquaintances, who lived two hundred miles apart."

October 6. **Barney McGinniskin** becomes the first Irish-American Boston police officer. Reporting to work on November 3, McGinniskin declares himself "fresh from the bogs of Ireland"—even though he had been in this country for 22 years. The appointment had been opposed by Marshal Francis Tukey and described as "a dangerous precedent to appoint a foreigner to stations of such trust," but McGinniskin is kept on—until three years later, when the "Know-Nothing" Party comes to power and he is dropped from the force.

1852

March 20. Harriet Beecher Stowe's ***Uncle Tom's Cabin; or, Life Among the Lowly*** is published by John P. Jewett of Boston. Stowe is the daughter of Rev. Lyman Beecher, who had been pastor of the Hanover Street Church in the North End in the 1820s. She wrote the novel while living in Maine, but it had a particularly dramatic effect on Bostonians. "We read ourselves into despair in that tragic book," Henry Wadsworth Longfellow complains. "It is too melancholy, and makes one's blood boil too hotly."

March 26. **Temple Ohabei Shalom** is dedicated on today's **Warrenton Street**. It is the first synagogue built in Boston and the second in New England after one in Newport, Rhode Island. The congregation was formed by Jewish immigrants from Poland in 1843 and moves to its current location on Beacon Street in Brookline in 1928.

April 1. The **Somerset Club** adopts its current name when it moves this year into the former David Hinckley house at today's **1 Somerset Street**. One of the most exclusive in the city, the club is an outgrowth of the Travelers Club and is first called the Tremont Club, then the Beacon Club. It moves to its current location in the former David Sears house at **42 Beacon Street** in 1872.

Police conveying the fugitive slave Sims to the ship that will return him to the South. Engraving from Gleason's Pictorial. (Courtesy of the Bostonian Society)

April 28. The Boston Fire Department, then located on **Court Square,** employs the first electric fire alarm system in the world when Box 1212 on **Causeway Street** is rung to signal the outbreak of a fire. The system was created by Dr. William F. Channing and Moses G. Farmer, and it consists of 40 miles of wire, 45 signal boxes, and 16 alarm bells. The system is moved to its current location at **59 The Fenway** in 1925, and some of its components are still in use.

November 20. The **Boston Music Hall** opens at today's **1 Hamilton Place.** Its opening prompts M.A. DeWolfe Howe to later write that at last "it was unnecessary to ask a visiting Jenny Lind to sing in the Fitchburg Railroad Station." The final scene of Henry James' *The Bostonians,* in which the hero declares: "even when exasperated, a Boston audience is not ungenerous" is set here. The building, now called the Orpheum Theatre, serves as the home of the Boston Symphony Orchestra until a new hall is constructed in 1900.*

1853
February 2. **Emma Snodgrass,** demonstrating for women's rights, causes a sensation by strolling through the streets of Boston dressed in men's clothing.

The **Chickering Piano Factory** opens at today's **791 Tremont Street in the South End.** Designed by Edwin Payson, it is the second largest building in the U.S. at the time, after the U.S. Capitol. The company later moves to Rochester and the building becomes the Piano Craft Guild, an artist housing and studio cooperative, in 1974.

October 4. Donald McKay's ***Great Republic*** is launched before 30,000 cheering spectators in East Boston. Because the shareholders are temperance advocates, the ship is christened with a bottle of water from Lake Cochituate. It is McKay's largest

ship and the largest on the seas at the time. But the development of steamships a few years later brings an end to the Clipper Ship era, and McKay sells his shipyard in 1869.

1854

January 9. **Dr. Jerome Van Crowninshield Smith**, a member of the newly formed "Know-Nothing" Party, is elected mayor of Boston. Later described as being "raised by accident to a mayoralty," Smith had formerly been Boston's port physician and had also written a book, *The Ways of Women*, in which he claimed that if women were elected to public office "they would have too much self-respect to . . . foist their imbecile relatives into office or vote to raise their own pay at the expense of the people overburdened by taxation."

May 24. Runaway slave **Anthony Burns** is captured in Boston. He is tried, found guilty, and ordered returned to his master in Virginia. Burns's supporters riot and a guard at the Suffolk County Courthouse on **Court Square** is killed on May 26. On June 2, 50,000 demonstrators line **State Street** as 2,000 militia, police, and federal soldiers escort Burns to the ship at Long Wharf that takes him back to the South. Burns subsequently has his freedom purchased by members of the Twelfth Baptist Church and returns to Boston before moving to Canada, where he becomes a minister.

May 26. The **Boston Police Department** is established. The force combines the day time Police and the Night Watch into one department that is modeled after the London police force. Police headquarters is initially located in an office in the Suffolk County Courthouse on **Court Square**. The current headquarters is located at **One Schroeder Plaza** in Roxbury.

1855

The **Saturday Club** is founded. Almost every prominent Boston-area man of letters eventually joins—including Ralph Waldo Emerson, Oliver Wendell Holmes, and James Russell Lowell. But Henry David Thoreau declines, writing: "They have got a club, the handle of which is in the Parker House at Boston, and with this they beat me from time to time, expecting to make me tender or minced meat." The group meets initially in a private dining room at the Parker House at **60 School Street** and later relocates to the Union Club at **8 Park Street,** where it continues today.

 The **Olympic Club of Boston** beats the Elm Tree Club in the first baseball game ever played in Boston on **Boston Common.** The teams play the "Massachusetts Game" or "New England Game," which involves a smaller ball and closer bases than the "New York Game" or "National Game," which is closer to the modern game of baseball.

The Parker House at 60 School Street, ca. 1892. (Courtesy of the Bostonian Society)

 October 5. The **Parker House** is opened by Harvey D. Parker at today's **60 School Street.** An outgrowth of Parker's Restaurant (est. 1832), it is the oldest continuously operated hotel in the U.S. The hotel's restaurant becomes known for its Boston cream pie and Parker House rolls, and for coining the term "scrod" for the whitefish catch of the day. Guests would include author Charles Dickens, generals Grant and Sherman, and actors Sarah Bernhardt and Edwin and John Wilkes Booth. Employees would include Malcolm X as a busboy and Ho Chi Minh as a pastry cook. The current building opens in 1927.

1856

 March 26. The first horsecar line in New England begins regular service between **Bowdoin Square** in Boston and Cambridgeport. Before being replaced by electric streetcars, there are an estimated 8,000 horsecars operating in the city. The last horsecar run is made along **Marlborough Street** on December 24, 1900.

 May 22. Senator **Charles Sumner** of Boston is beaten with a walking stick by U.S. Rep. Preston Brooks of South Carolina on the floor of the Senate in the Capitol in Washington. Sumner had criticized Brooks's uncle, Sen. Andrew Butler of South Carolina, for supporting slavery in a speech he delivered a few days before entitled "The Crimes Against Kansas." Sumner is badly injured but welcomed by a large crowd of people when he returns to Boston on November 3 to begin his convalescence.

1857

January 4. **John Brown** makes the first of several visits to consult with supporters in Boston, including members of the "Secret Six" (New Englanders Thomas Wentworth Higginson, Samuel Gridley Howe, Theodore Parker, Franklin Sanborn, and George Stearns, and New Yorker Gerrit Smith). He meets with Howe and Parker, probably at Howes's office at **20 Bromfield Street,** and speaks to a number of Boston and Boston-area congregations. Although Brown's raid at Harper's Ferry, West Virginia, on October 16, 1859, is denounced as "misguided" by William Lloyd Garrison in *The Liberator*, on the day of his execution Boston church bells are rung and sermons are preached in his honor.

$ *August 24.* The **Panic of 1857** is sparked by the failure of the New York branch of the Ohio Life Insurance and Trust Company. Boston banks stop specie payments for 60 days, and the depression that follows diminishes Boston's standing as a commercial and business center. The result, according to Thomas H. O'Connor, was that: "In haste—indeed, in panic—the North's business interests adopted a much more tolerant attitude toward the South in general and the slavery issue in particular."

October 27. The first issue of *The Atlantic Monthly* appears. Founded by members of the Magazine, or Atlantic Club (most of whose members also belong to the Saturday Club), it is published by James Fields from the Old Corner Bookstore at today's **3 School Street.** James Russell Lowell, the first editor, declares the magazine will be "free without being fanatical," its pages open to "all available talents of all shades of opinion." The magazine prints the first stories of Mark Twain, Henry James, and Ernest Hemingway. For many years, the magazine is located at **8 Arlington Street**. It is today published from Washington, DC.

1858

April. The major filling of the **Back Bay** begins. It is accomplished by constructing a nine-mile railroad line from Needham on which locomotives pull trains made up of 35 gravel cars every hour, 24 hours a day, six days a week, for the next five years—then less frequently after that. The made land reaches **Clarendon Street** by 1860 and **Exeter Street** by 1870 and the project is completed in 1876. The first houses are built in 1859. Lewis Mumford later declares that it was "in the Back Bay that Boston first established itself as one of the centers of world culture in the arts and sciences."

Oliver Wendell Holmes coins the phrase **"Hub of the Universe"** in his column "The Autocrat of the Breakfast-Table" in *The Atlantic Monthly*. Holmes recounts the story of a man repeating the saying: "Boston State House is the hub of the solar system. You couldn't pry that out of a Boston man if you had the tire of all creation straightened out for a crowbar."

1859

March 7. Ten-year-old Thomas Whall, a Catholic and student at the Eliot School at **16 Charter Street** in the North End, refuses to say the "Protestant" version of the Lord's Prayer. After refusing again a week later, Whall is beaten by his teacher. Hundreds of other Catholic students join in his protest and they are all expelled. Whall subsequently receives praise and tributes—including gold medals—from Catholic parishes and schools around the country.

Engraving by an unknown artist prior to the filling in of the Back Bay. (Courtesy of the Bostonian Society)

1860

October 18. The **Prince of Wales** (the future Edward VII) visits Boston, prompting a daylong celebration in his honor. A military review is held on **Boston Common** in the morning, a musical festival at the Music Hall at **1 Hamilton Place** in the afternoon, and a ball at the Academy of Music at today's **1 Federal Street** in the evening. For the ball, 1,100 tickets are printed for "ladies and gentlemen." An additional 525 for "ladies only." Supper is served at midnight and the dancing continues until 4:30 a.m.

December 18. **Henry Wadsworth Longfellow's** poem **"Paul Revere's Ride"** is first published on the front page of the *Boston Evening Transcript.* Longfellow had climbed up into the steeple of the Old North Church on April 5 and began work on the poem a day later. The poem next appears in the January 1861 edition of *The Atlantic Monthly,* then as "The Landlord's Tale" in *Tales of a Wayside Inn,* published in 1863. In 1868, Lexington town historian Charles Hudson comments on the poem's historical inaccuracies: "We have heard of poetic license, but have always understood this to be confined to modes of expression and regions of the imagination, and should not extend to historic facts . . . when poets pervert matters of history . . . they should be restrained, as Revere was in his midnight ride."

1861

Oliver Wendell Holmes's novel *Elsie Venner: A Romance of Destiny* is published. The novel popularizes the term "Boston Brahmin," which Holmes calls "the harmless, inoffensive, untitled aristocracy." It also contains the passage: "Boston Brahmins . . . with their houses by Bulfinch, their monopoly of Beacon Street, their ancestral portraits and Chinese porcelains, humanitarianism, Unitarian faith in the march of the mind, Yankee shrewdness, and New England exclusiveness."

September 30. **Elizabeth Palmer Peabody** opens the first successful kindergarten school in the U.S. at what was then **24½ Winter Street.** Modeled after the "children's garden" movement promoted by German educator Friedrich Frobel, the

Robert Gould Shaw
and the 54th Regiment
Memorial on
the Boston Common,
by Augustus
Saint-Gaudens.
(Courtesy of the
Bostonian Society)

school later moves to **15 Pinckney Street** on Beacon Hill, a building that has since been demolished.

1862

The **New England Hospital for Women and Children** opens at **60 Pleasant Street**. The first hospital in the U.S. run and staffed by women, its mission is "to provide for women medical aide of competent physicians of their own sex." Dr. Marie Zakrzewska is the first director. The hospital moves to its current location at today's **55 Dimock Street** in Roxbury and becomes the Dimock Community Health Center in 1969.

1863

January 1. A series of events—attended by both blacks and whites—is held to celebrate the implementation of the Emancipation Proclamation. At the Music Hall on **Hamilton Place**, Beethoven's *Fifth Symphony* and Handel's *Hallelujah Chorus* are performed and Emerson recites the "Boston Hymn," which includes the lines: "To-day unbind the captive./So only are ye unbound;/Lift up a people from the dust./ Trump of their rescue, sound!" At Tremont Temple at today's **88 Tremont Street**, Frederick Douglass wrote later: "I never saw Joy before. Men, women, young and old were up; hats and bonnets were in the air." On **Boston Common**, a 100-gun salute is fired.

May 28. The **Massachusetts 54th Regiment** marches past the State House at **24 Beacon Street** on its way to Battery Wharf for a voyage to South Carolina. The first all African-American volunteer company to fight for the Union, it is led by 26-year-old Col. **Robert Gould Shaw**. Shaw, two other officers, and 31 soldiers are killed in an attack on Fort Wagner in Charleston Harbor, South Carolina, on July 18. *July 14.* A draft riot breaks out in the North End, after a woman is presented with a draft notice for her husband outside their home at 146 Prince Street. Thousands of mostly Irish immigrants take part, and soldiers from Fort Independence along with recent Harvard graduates holding their class reunion at the Parker House are called upon to restore order. Two days before the riot, the *Boston Herald* had declared: "The draft is received in this State without the faintest show of opposition, so far as we have learned."

An etiquette pamphlet published in Boston advises: "The perfect hostess will see to it that the works of male and females authors be properly separated on her bookshelves. Their proximity unless they are married should not be tolerated."

The **Boston Eight-Hour League** is founded by **George McNeil** and **Ira Steward**, who later writes: "Men who labor excessively are robbed of all ambition to ask for anything more than will satisfy their bodily necessities, while those who labor moderately have time to cultivate tastes and create wants in addition to mere physical comforts."

Boston City Hospital Administration Building, ca. 1865–1875. (Courtesy of the Bostonian Society)

1864

March 1. **Rebecca Lee** becomes the first African-American woman doctor in the U.S. when she graduates from the **New England Female Medical College** at **133 E. Springfield Street** in the South End. She serves as a nurse during the Civil War, then establishes a practice with her husband, Dr. Arthur Crumpler, at their home at **67 Joy Street** on Beacon Hill.

May 24. **Boston City Hospital** is dedicated at today's **818 Harrison Avenue** in the South End. Designed by Gridley J.F. Bryant, its mission is to serve "the honest, temperate and industrious poor." A new hospital is built by the city in 1994, but the hospital is subsequently turned over to Boston University and becomes the Boston Medical Center in 1996.

June 1. The **Museum of Science** (originally Boston Society of Natural History) opens at **234 Berkeley Street**. The first of its kind in New England, it was organized in 1830. It moves to its current location on the **Charles River Dam** in 1951.

The first annual **Boston Schoolboy Parades** is held, a year after the state legislature recommends making military drills part of every school curriculum for boys over 12 years old. The parades of high school military marching bands attract as many as 300,000 spectators and continue until 1960.

The National Peace Jubilee, from a stereograph of the interior of the Coliseum in Copley Square. (Courtesy of the Bostonian Society)

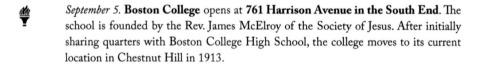

September 5. **Boston College** opens at **761 Harrison Avenue in the South End**. The school is founded by the Rev. James McElroy of the Society of Jesus. After initially sharing quarters with Boston College High School, the college moves to its current location in Chestnut Hill in 1913.

1865

February 20. **Massachusetts Institute of Technology** opens, with a class of 15 students, in rented rooms at **16 Summer Street**. Originally known as Boston Tech, the school moves across the Charles River to Cambridge in 1916.

February. Boston lawyer **John Swett Rock** becomes the first African-American to practice law before the U.S. Supreme Court and the first to speak before the U.S. House of Representatives.

April 15. News of the assassination of President Lincoln the day before reaches Boston, resulting in an outpouring of grief. Boston Harbor is closed while a manhunt is conducted for **John Wilkes Booth,** who had visited Boston 10 days earlier, stayed at the Parker House at **3 School Street,** and practiced his shooting at Edward Rold's Pistol Gallery on **Chapman Place.**

September 18. **Old City Hall** is dedicated at today's **43 School Street**. Designed by Gridley J. F. Bryant and Arthur Gilman in the French second empire style, it is described by author Edwin O'Connor in *The Last Hurrah* as "a lunatic pile of a building: a great, grim resolutely ugly dust-catcher." The building is converted to commercial uses in 1971.

1866

October 15. The leveling of **Fort Hill** begins. Destruction of the 80-foot, 20-acre hill is completed in July 1872 and the fill used to create Atlantic Avenue and raise the Bay

Village area. The project is as much a slum clearance operation as an expansion of the city. In the 1840s, a committee studying the area had declared: "Here is a density of population surpassed, probably, in few places in the civilized world."

The **L Street Bath House** opens at today's **1663 Columbia Road** in South Boston. The first free municipal public baths in the U.S., its current art deco building opens in 1931. The bathhouse is home to the **L Street Brownies,** who begin their annual tradition of a New Year's Day swim in the ocean in 1904.

1867

February 11. **Boston Conservatory** is founded. The music school moves to its current location at the former Boston Medical Library building at **8 The Fenway** in 1936.
February 18. The **New England Conservatory** is founded. Originally located in rented rooms in the Music Hall on **Hamilton Place,** the school moves to the former St. James Hotel at **11 East Newton Street** in the South End in 1882, and to its current location at **290 Huntington Avenue** in 1902.

March. The **Calumet & Hecla Consolidated Copper Company** is founded to develop a copper mine in Michigan that had been discovered by Edwin Hulbert. Control of the mine is soon wrested from Hulbert by **Quincy A. Shaw** and **Alexander Agassiz,** which prompts Hulbert to later write: "In my younger days, I became strangely, confidently, and I may add, foolishly, impressed [with] the significance of an oft quoted phrase, which read, in this way, 'The solid men of Boston.'" The mines soon produce half the copper in the U.S. and, according to Bliss Perry, "the unwritten history of the public and private benefactions—scientific, artistic, philanthropic—made possible by Calumet & Hecla, and its influence upon certain family histories is a theme worthy of Balzac."

1868

January. In an article in the *North American Review,* **Charles Francis Adams** bemoans Boston's failure to continue to grow as a commercial center. "The merchant and the manufacturer were no longer to move forward with equal steps," he complains, "Boston. . . in spite of her wealth and prestige, her intrinsic worth and deserved reputation, her superficial conceit and real cultivation, failed to solve the enigma—did not rise to the height of the great argument. The new era found her wedded to the old, and her eyes, dimmed with experiences of the past, could not credit the brilliant visions of the future. . . She has lost much of her influence and all of her prestige."

November 19. **New England Woman Suffrage Association** is founded by Lucy Stone, Henry Blackwell, and Thomas Wentworth Higginson. Julia Ward Howe is the first president. It is considered the first major political society whose goal is women's suffrage and becomes a national organization, the American Woman's Suffrage Association, in 1869 and then the National American Woman Suffrage Association in 1890.

1869

May. **Boston University** is incorporated. Founded in 1839 by the New England

Crowds at the South End Grounds watching the Boston Nationals baseball club. (Courtesy of the Bostonian Society)

Friends of Improved Theological Training by Methodists, the school was initially located in various places in northern New England, then moved to Boston as the Boston Theological Seminary in 1867. It subsequently becomes the first university in the U.S. to admit women to all of its departments in 1873. Located initially on Beacon Hill, it moves to its current campus along **Commonwealth Avenue** in 1948.

June 15. Patrick Sarsfield Gilmore's **National Peace Jubilee** opens in a specially built coliseum in today's **Copley Square**. The first concert is performed by a 1,000-member orchestra, accompanied by a 10,000-voice choir and 100 Boston firemen beating anvils, playing before an audience of 50,000 people, which the *New York Times* calls "the largest, most eager throng that ever awaited admission to an American place of entertainment."

July. **Children's Hospital** opens at **9 Rutland Square** in the South End. The 20-bed hospital is the third children's hospital in the U.S. after those in Philadelphia and Chicago. It moves a number of times before settling at its current location at **300 Longwood Avenue** in 1914.

1870

March 8. Forty-four women, led by abolitionist and women's rights advocates **Angelina** and **Sarah Grimké**, cast the first votes by women in the U.S. when they attempt to vote in a municipal election in Hyde Park. Their ballots are later discarded.

May 10. **Julia Ward Howe** issues a "**Mother's Day of Peace Proclamation**" in an effort to unite mothers against war and for disarmament. Inspired by Ann Jarvis, a West Virginia nurse who tried to improve sanitation through what she called "Mother's

Ruins on Beacon Street after the Great Boston Fire, 1872.
(Courtesy of the Bostonian Society)

Work Days," Howe's proclamation reads: "Arise, the women of this day! . . . Say firmly, 'We will not have great questions decided by irrelevant agencies, our husbands shall not come to us, reeking of carnage, for caresses and applause. Our sons shall not be taken from us to unlearn all that we have been able to teach them of charity, mercy and patience." The first Mother's Day is celebrated in 1908 in the West Virginia church where Ann Jarvis taught Sunday School and it is declared a national holiday in 1914.

John Boyle O'Reilly arrives in Boston. As a soldier in the British army, he had been convicted of treason for trying to recruit other Irish-born soldiers to join the cause of Irish independence and was sentenced to prison in Australia, but he made a daring escape the year before. Arriving in Boston, he is befriended by Patrick Collins, who finds him a job as a reporter for *The Pilot*.

1871

The **Hotel Vendome** opens at **160 Commonwealth Avenue** in the Back Bay. Designed by William G. Preston in the French second empire style, it becomes the largest hotel in the city after an addition is constructed in 1881. It is the first hotel in the U.S. lit by electricity, the installation of which is personally inspected by Thomas Edison in 1882. Guests would include Presidents Grant and Cleveland, P.T. Barnum, Sarah Bernhardt, Mark Twain, and Oscar Wilde. The hotel closes in 1970 and the building is heavily damaged by a fire in which nine Boston firefighters lose their lives on June 17, 1972. It is transformed into a residential building in 1975.

1872

March 4. The first issue of the *Boston Globe* appears. **Charles H. Taylor** becomes publisher a year later and the Taylor family maintains ownership until selling the paper to the *New York Times* in 1993. Located initially at **236–238 Washington Street**,

Cathedral of the Holy Cross,
1400 Washington Street, ca. 1875.
(Courtesy of the Bostonian Society)

the paper moves to its current location at **135 Morrissey Boulevard** in Dorchester in 1958.

March. The **Arnold Arboretum** is established by Harvard University at **125 The Arborway** in Jamaica Plain. The first in the U.S., the now 265-acre park contains more than 6,500 living plants. It is funded by New Bedford businessman and horticulturist James Arnold on land donated by scientific farmer Benjamin Bussey. Harvard turns the property over to the City of Boston in 1882, which leases it back to the university for 1,000 years at $1 per year—with an option to renew under the same terms.

November 9. The **Great Boston Fire** breaks out in the basement of a hoop skirt Factory at **83–85 Summer Street**. The fire burns for four days, kills 14 people, and destroys 776 buildings on 65 acres. The contents of many bank vaults in the area are reduced to ash, prompting Oliver Wendell Holmes to comment: "I saw the fire eating its way straight toward my deposits." The calamity forces insurance companies to reorganize and prompts adoption of more stringent building code regulations, but Boston Mayor Henry L. Pierce rejects suggestions that the city use the opportunity to rearrange Boston's confusing downtown streets into a more cohesive pattern.

1873

Ellen Swallow Richards becomes the first woman graduate of MIT and the first woman in the U.S. to receive a bachelor's degree in chemistry. Admitted as a special student and nicknamed "Ellencyclopedia," she later teaches at the college and becomes a pioneer in the field of sanitary engineering.

$ The **Abattoir** opens along 1,000 feet of the Charles River off **Market**

Street in Brighton. Construction of the 60-acre facility was ordered by the Massachusetts legislature due to public health concerns, and the new building relocates the more than 20 slaughterhouses that had been operating in the area into one place. One of those was owned by Gustavus Swift and becomes the largest in the country before moving to Chicago. The Abattoir closes in 1956.

Massachusetts College of Art and Design opens in rented rooms at **33 Pemberton Square**. Originally the Massachusetts Normal Art School, it is created to train teachers to teach students industrial drawing to boost the state's textile and metal-working industries. It becomes the first and only freestanding public art college in the U.S. when it moves to its own building at its current location at **621 Huntington Avenue** in 1983.

1874
January 5. Brighton, Charlestown, and West Roxbury (including Jamaica Plain and Roslindale) are annexed to Boston.

Four women—Ann Adeline Badger, Lucretia Crocker, Abigail Williams May, and Lucia Peabody—are elected to the Boston School Committee after the Massachusetts legislature passes a law making women eligible to serve on school committees in the commonwealth.

1875
January 1. The **Steaming Kettle** contest is held by the Oriental Tea Company at today's **65 Court Street**. Contestants are asked to guess the capacity of the giant kettle hanging outside the company's door. A crowd estimated at 15,000 turns out to witness the results. After eight boys and a man in a tall silk hat climb out of the kettle, eight people are declared the winners for having correctly guessed the exact capacity of the pot (227 gallons, 2 quarts, 1 pint, and 3 gills). The eight share the first prize—a chest of 40 pounds of tea. The kettle remains today—hanging, ironically, outside a Starbuck's.

Boston's **Chinatown** is first established in today's **Ping-On Alley**. Its residents are Chinese workers, living in tents, who were brought from California to break a strike at a shoe factory in North Adams, Massachusetts, and then moved on to Boston in search of work. The community expands south of Kneeland Street when the Atlantic Avenue elevated line is taken down in 1942.

Charles Waite, first baseman for a Boston amateur team, uses the first baseball glove. The invention is not immediately popular with other players, who hesitate to join what would be derided by newspapers as the "kid glove aristocracy."

December 8. The **Cathedral of the Holy Cross** is dedicated at **1400 Washington Street** in the South End. Designed by Patrick C. Keeley, it is one of the largest Gothic cathedrals in the world. The basement chapel contains the altar from the first Boston cathedral on Franklin Street, and the arch separating the vestibule from the interior uses bricks from the ruins of the Ursuline Convent in Charlestown, which was burned down by an anti-Catholic mob. Two towers that were part of the original design are never built.

December 15. The **New Old South Church** (Third Church in Boston) is dedicated at **645 Boylston Street** in the Back Bay. It is built from Roxbury pudding stone and designed in the Italian Gothic style by the architects Cummings and Sears, who include their own likenesses in the piers that support the building's porch. The tower, which began to tilt almost as soon as it is was constructed, is torn down to prevent its collapse and rebuilt in 1940.

1876

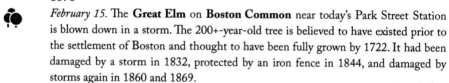

February 15. The **Great Elm** on **Boston Common** near today's Park Street Station is blown down in a storm. The 200+-year-old tree is believed to have existed prior to the settlement of Boston and thought to have been fully grown by 1722. It had been damaged by a storm in 1832, protected by an iron fence in 1844, and damaged by storms again in 1860 and 1869.

March 10. **Alexander Graham Bell** invents the telephone at **5 Exeter Place**, near the corner of today's **Harrison Avenue** and **Lafayette Place**. A member of the Boston University faculty on sabbatical, Bell had set up his laboratory in a boardinghouse there in order to work in secrecy. After accidentally spilling acid on his clothes, he transmits the first intelligible speech ("Mr. Watson, come here. I want to see you.") to his assistant, Thomas A. Watson, who is in another room. Bell had earlier transmitted sounds, but not a distinguishable human voice, in Charles Williams's shop at **109 Court Street**, on the site of today's JFK Building Plaza, on June 2, 1875.

April 29. The **Boston Braves**, a team in the new National League, lose to the Hartford team 3–2 in 10 innings in their first home game at the South End Grounds on the site of today's **Ruggles Station**. Initially without a name, the team becomes known, as the Red Caps, Beaneaters, Doves and the Rustlers before becoming the Braves in 1912.

The **Appalachian Mountain Club** is founded in Boston by **Edward Pickering** and 33 others. Its goal is to promote outdoor activities and the protection of the environment. The club initially holds monthly meetings at **9 Park Street** and its current headquarters at **5 Joy Street** on Beacon Hill. The club opens its first trail at Tuckerman's Ravine in 1879 and its first hut at Madison Spring in 1888.

1877

January 4. The **Footlight Club** is founded by Caroline Morse at the German Theatre on **Boylston Street** in Jamaica Plain. The oldest community theater in the U.S., its purpose is "to promote friendly and social intercourse, and to furnish pleasant and useful entertainment by the aid of the drama." The company moves to Eliot Hall at **7A Eliot Street** in 1878.

February 9. **Trinity Church** is dedicated at **233 Clarendon Street**. Designed by H.H. Richardson in the Romanesque style, the church is built on filled land and rests on more than 4,000 wooden piles that must be kept from drying out. The interior design is by John LaFarge. Van Wyck Brooks later describes the building's significance as "the break of the Boston mind with its Puritan past."

The **Women's Educational and Industrial Union** is founded by Dr. Harriet Crisby and others, initially at **4 Park Street**. Its goal is "to promote the educational, industrial, and social advancement of women," and it provides free legal advice, establishes an employment bureau, and begins the first credit union in the U.S. in 1913. The organization mergers with the Crittenton-Hastings House to become the **Women's Crittenton Union** and is now located at **1 Washington Mall**.

Parker Bailey becomes the first African-American graduate of **Boston Latin School**. He goes on to graduate from Harvard College and become a high school teacher in Washington, DC.

The **Longwood Cricket Club** is organized on the David Sears estate, which is named "Longwood" after the name of Napoleon's home in exile on St. Helena, and was located on today's **Brookline Avenue**. Formed to promote cricket, it soon becomes more of a tennis club and moves to its current location in Chestnut Hill in 1922.

1878

February 11. The **Boston Bicycle Club** is founded by G.B. Woodward and others at **87 Boylston Street**. The first bicycle club in the U.S., it adopts uniforms consisting of a gray jacket, shirt, breeches, and stocking and a blue cap.

May. The **New England Watch and Ward Society** is organized at a meeting in the basement of the Park Street Church at **1 Park Street**. The organization is founded "to remove commercialized temptations to vice and crime" in Boston, and under the leadership of longtime secretary J. Franklin Chase it is able to ban scores of what it calls "indecent" books from being sold in Boston, including Theodore Dreiser's *An American Tragedy*, Sinclair Lewis's *Elmer Gantry*, John Dos Passos's *Manhattan Transfer*, and Ernest Hemingway's *The Sun Also Rises*. Unsuccessful in its attempt to ban the book *Forever Amber* in 1948, the organization's power wanes thereafter.

The Church of Our Lady of Perpetual Help opens at **1525 Tremont Street** on Mission Hill. Popularly known as **Mission Church**, it is designed by Schickel & Ditmar in the Romanesque style and built from Roxbury pudding stone taken from Coleman's Quarry across the street. Twin 250-foot towers, designed by Franz Joseph Untersee, are added in 1910.

December 24. **Horatio J. Homer** is appointed the first African-American officer in the Boston Police Department. A resident of Brighton, Homer serves in the commissioner's office at Pemberton Square during the week and on Sundays walks a beat between Copley Square and Charles Street.

December. **Frederick Law Olmsted** is hired as an advisor by the Boston Park Commissioners to develop what becomes known as the **Emerald Necklace**, a 9-mile,

The Museum of Fine Arts at Copley Square, in a photograph taken between 1876 and 1890.
(Courtesy of the Bostonian Society)

thousand+-acre chain of parks. In his *Notes on the Plan of Franklin Park and Related Matters* in 1885, Olmsted declares that "the beauty of the park should be . . . the beauty of the fields, the meadow, the prairie, of the green pastures, and the still waters. What we want to gain is tranquillity and rest to the mind."

1879

 April 12. The **Church of Christ Scientist** is founded by **Mary Baker Eddy**. The congregation meets first in her parlor, then in various rented rooms and halls. The First Church of Christ Scientist (now known as "the chapel"), designed by Franklin Welch, opens near **Massachusetts Avenue** in 1905. Its replacement (now known as "the basilica"), designed by Brigham and Beman, opens adjacent to it in 1906. The *Christian Science Monitor* newspaper publishes its first edition on November 25, 1908.

 The **Hong Far Low Restaurant** becomes the first Chinese restaurant in Boston when it opens at **36½ Harrison Avenue**. The restaurant closes in 1960.

1880

 After the annexation of Brighton, Charlestown, Dorchester, Roxbury, and West Roxbury (including Jamaica Plain), Boston's population is 362,839. It is the fifth largest city in the U.S.

 The **"three-decker"** tenement begins to be constructed in Boston. Built on a small plot, the design of the building allows light for all three units and provides the home owner with rental income. New housing codes end construction of the traditional three-decker after 1926.

 In *The Perfect Brahmin*, John Jay Chapman describes the social scene of the era:

Swan Boats on the lagoon in the Public Garden, in a photograph taken in 1941. (Courtesy of the Bostonian Society)

"Evening receptions were regarded as a natural form of amusement; people stood in a pack, and ate and drank, and talked volubly till midnight. And they enjoyed it too. There was a zest in it. I don't why the world has become so dull of recent years, and society is so insipid. People in Boston in the Eighties knew how to enjoy themselves."

Houghton, Mifflin Company is formed by the merger of the former Ticknor & Fields and the Riverside Press. Among its best-known books would be J.R.R. Tolkien's *Lord of the Rings* trilogy, James Agee and Walker Evans's *Let Us Now Praise Famous Men*, Rachel Carson's *Silent Spring*, Esther Forbes's *Johnny Tremain*, and Roger Tory Peterson's bird guides. The company establishes a profitable textbook division and begins publishing children's books—including H.A. and Margaret Rey's *Curious George* series—in 1937. Located for many years at **2 Park Street**, the company moves to **222 Berkeley Street** in the 1990s.

September 17. Boston celebrates its 250th birthday. Two parades are held—one during the day, one at night. Speaking at the Old South Church, Boston Mayor **Frederick O. Prince** declares: "Scarcely a feature of the landscape remains to tell us how nature looked before she was subdued by civilization. The sea has been converted into land; the hills have been leveled—the valleys filled up, the sites of the Indian wigwams are now those of the palaces of our merchant princes, and where 'the wild fox dug his hole unscared', art has reared her beautiful temples for the worship of God and the dissemination of learning."

1881

Clark's Boston Blue Book is published. Subtitled *The Elite Private Address and Carriage Directory, Ladies Visiting and Shopping Guide for Boston, Brookline, Cambridge, Jamaica Plain and Charlestown District*, it is published annually thereafter.

September 6. "**Yellow Day**" occurs in Boston. The air is clouded as a result of forest fires in Michigan and Canada, and the temperature reaches 102 degrees, one of the hottest days in the city's history.

October 22. The **Boston Symphony Orchestra** makes its debut performance at the Boston Music Hall at **1 Hamilton Place**. It is founded by **Major Henry Lee Higginson** to provide "the best music at low prices, such as may be found in all the large European cities, or even in the smaller musical centres of Germany." The orchestra moves to a new building in 1900.*

1882

January 31. **Oscar Wilde** lectures at the Boston Music Hall at **1 Hamilton Place**. In his talk, Wilde declares that Boston is "the only city to influence thought in Europe . . . in Boston are the elements of a great civilized city; a permanent intellectual tradition." But Harvard students, in an attempt to mock Wilde, had threatened to attend the lecture wearing "dress coat, knee breeches and silk stockings, with lilies in their buttonholes." An editor at the *Boston Transcript* later explains Wilde's less-than-warm reception by writing: "There are some things that can be done in New York that cannot be done in Boston."

February 7. **John L. Sullivan** KO's Paddy Ryan in the ninth round to win the U.S. bare-knuckles heavyweight boxing championship in Mississippi City, Mississippi. Born in Roxbury, Sullivan becomes known as, "The Boston Strong Boy," and once boasted, "I can lick any man in the house," at the Dudley Opera House at **111 Dudley Street**. He loses the heavyweight championship to James J. Corbett in a 21-round fight in New Orleans in the first title fight in which gloves are worn on September 7, 1892.

F. J. Doyle's & Co. opens at today's **3484 Washington Street** in Jamaica Plain. Founded by brothers Francis and Barney Doyle, it is expanded in 1907 to include the Braddock Cafe. The Doyle brothers' nephew, Bill, sells the business to the Burke brothers–Ed, Bill, and Gerard–in 1971, and his family continues to operate the tavern today.

1883

May 1. **Franklin Park** (originally West Roxbury Park) opens in Roxbury. The park is renamed Franklin Park in 1884 in anticipation of being able to use the fund that Benjamin Franklin left to the City of Boston for development of the park. A decision that the funds cannot be used for the park is made in 1891, but the name remains. The park is named the second most beautiful park in the world after one in Berlin in 1927.

The **Clover Club** is founded by a group of Irish-Americans including Thomas Riley for "the social enjoyment of its members," many of whom are excluded from the city's exclusive social clubs. The club never establishes a headquarters and instead holds annual dinners that include both serious speeches and performances of parodies of popular songs.

October 1. The *Count of Monte Cristo*, starring **James O'Neill**, opens at the Globe Theatre at today's **364 Washington Street**. O'Neill performs in the play thousands of times during his career and was the model for the father in his son Eugene's play *Long Day's Journey into Night*.

1884

December 9. **Hugh O'Brien** is elected the first Irish-Catholic mayor of Boston. Born in Ireland, O'Brien emigrated to Boston with his family at age five, quit school at twelve to earn his living, became a newspaper publisher. He pleases—and surprises—the Yankee business establishment in Boston with his personal and fiscal moderation as mayor.

Portrait of Frederick Law Olmsted. (Courtesy of the National Park Service, Frederick Law Olmsted National Historic Site)

The **Cyclorama Building** opens at **539 Tremont Street** in the South End. Designed by Cummings and Sears, it is built to house the 50'x400' cylindrical painting *The Battle of Gettysburg* by French artist Paul Dominique Philippoteaux. Although the cylindrical design of the building was common at the time, it is one of only three such buildings remaining in North America. The building becomes home to the Boston Flower Exchange in 1923 and the Boston Center for the Arts in 1970.

1885

July 11. The first **Boston Pops** concert is performed by the Boston Symphony Orchestra at the Boston Music Hall at **1 Hamilton Place**. Originally called the Promenade Concerts, its subsequent name comes from a popular march tune ("The Pops") performed at the first concert. The concerts are described as "light music of the best class." The series is renamed the Symphony Hall Pops at its Symphony Hall debut on May 6, 1901, and the name is later shortened to the Boston Pops.

December 20. The **Hendricks Club** is founded, established on the corner of **Causeway** and **Lowell Streets** by **Martin Lomasney**. It moves to **9 Green Street** in 1908. Known as "The Mahatma," Lomasney is one of the most powerful ward bosses in the city and once declares: "The great mass of people are interested in only three things—food, clothing, and shelter. A politician in a district such as mine sees to it that his people get these things. If he does, then he doesn't have to worry about their loyalty and support."

1886

Oliver Wendell Holmes writes a smug paean to the city: "What better provision can be made for mortal man than such as our own Boston can offer its wealthy children? A palace on Commonwealth Avenue or on Beacon Street; a country-place at

Framingham or Lenox; a seaside residence at Nahant, Beverly Farms, Newport, or Bar Harbor; a pew at Trinity or King's Chapel; a tomb at Mount Auburn or Forest Hills; with the prospect of a memorial stained-window after his lamented demise,—is not that a pretty programme to offer a candidate for human existence?"

September. **B.F. Keith** and **E.F. Albee** introduce **vaudeville** at the Bijou Theatre at today's **545 Washington Street**. It is family-oriented entertainment that includes song, dance, and comedy. Performers here would include George M. Cohan, Harry Houdini, and the comedy team of Weber and W.C. Fields.

1887

March 14. The **Bussey Bridge Disaster** takes place at **South Street** and **Archdale Road** in Roslindale. It is the worst railroad accident in the U.S. up to that time. Twenty-three people are killed and more than 100 are injured when a commuter train from Dedham derails on the Bussey Bridge.

November 25. **Boston Latin** beats **Boston English** 16–0 on Boston Common in the first of what becomes the oldest continuous high school football rivalry in the U.S. The games are played today at Harvard Stadium.

1888

The **Mount Bellevue Water Tower** is built on **Bellevue Hill** in West Roxbury. It is the tallest point in Boston at 325 feet above sea level. The wooden building is replaced by a Romanesque revival-style granite structure in 1916 and by the current metal tank in 1956.

John Singer Sargent holds his first solo exhibition at the St. Botolph Club, then located at **2 Newbury Street**. The show includes a portrait of Isabella Stewart Gardner that is considered so sensual that her husband, Jack Gardner, orders it to be removed it from public view. Although it is later hung at Fenway Court, Mrs. Gardner prohibits it from being shown until after her death.

August 28. **Friederich Engels** visits Boston to see his nephew, Willie, who works for the Boston and Providence Railroad. Engels writes in his diary: "Boston is just a village, sprawling far and wide, more human than New York City."

1889

January 1. The first electric streetcar operates in Boston, running from the Allston car barn through Brookline to Park Square. Boston becomes the first major city in the U.S. to electrify its entire system in 1896.

The **Ames Building** opens at **1 Court Street**. Designed by Shepley, Rutan, and Coolidge in the Romanesque style, it is the tallest building in New England at 13 stories and is built just prior to the introduction of steel-framed construction. The building is converted into a hotel in 2009.

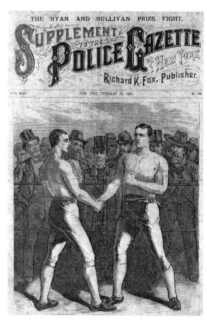

The **Charlesbank** becomes the first "open air gymnasium" in the U.S. when it opens on the Charles River in the West End. The 10-acre park was conceived by Dr. Paul Dudley White and designed by Frederick Law Olmsted. Originally only for men, the parks adds a women's gymnasium, screened by shrubbery to provide "the seclusion desirable for the sex that uses them," in 1891.

Hecht House is founded by Mrs. Jacob (Lina) Hecht, initially on **Hanover Street** in the North End. Originally called the Hebrew Industrial School for Girls, it moves to its own building on **Bulfinch Place** in the West End in 1922 and provides recreational and occupational opportunities for both boys and girls in that neighborhood. The organization moves to Dorchester in 1936 and closes in 1970.

Ryan and Sullivan prize fight, from the cover of the Supplement to the Police Gazette. (Courtesy of the Bostonian Society)

October 16. **Helen Keller** enters the Perkins Institution for the Blind, then located on **Broadway** and **H Street** in South Boston. Keller had been left blind, deaf, and mute by illness when she was 19 months old, but thanks to the instruction she receives in Boston she learns to read and speak. Keller graduates from Radcliffe College in 1904.

1890

Castle Island is transferred by the federal government to the City of Boston. A wooden causeway connecting it to Marine Park in South Boston is opened in 1892 and a roadway in 1932. Fort Independence is reactivated during World War II as a facility to demagnetize ship hulls to avoid German mines.

December 9. **Nathan Matthews Jr.** is elected mayor of Boston for the first of four consecutive terms. A graduate of Harvard and Harvard Law School and a lecturer in municipal government there, he is later described by John Galvin as "the most astute student of city government to hold the office."

1891

The **"Composer Streets"** are laid out in Roslindale. Located in an area formerly called "Gypsy Hill," they include Brahms, Haydn, Liszt, and Mendelssohn Streets. Originally private roads, they become public ways in 1929.

F. J. Doyle's Tavern, Jamaica Plain, today. (Photograph by Richard Tourangeau)

South End House (originally Andover House) is founded at **20 Union Park** by theology professor William Jewett Tucker. It is the first settlement house in Boston and the fourth in the U.S. Dennison House in South Cove, the North End Union, and the Elizabeth Peabody House in the West End are founded soon after.

The *Boston Social Register* list of 8,000 families includes less than a dozen Catholic families and only one Jewish family, that of Louis D. Brandeis.

William Dean Howells leaves Boston for New York. Despite having written, "The Bostonian who leaves Boston ought to be condemned to perpetual exile," Howells now declares that Boston was "no life but death-in-life."

1892

September 8. The Pledge of Allegiance is first published in *The Youth's Companion* magazine, with offices at **201 Columbus Avenue**. Written by Francis Bellamy and edited by James Upham, it is part of an issue celebrating the 400th anniversary of Columbus's discovery of America.

The **Vincent Club** is organized, with a clubhouse at **71 Brimmer Street**. The women's club organizes an annual theatrical production to benefit the Vincent Hospital that includes a precision dance routine known as the "Vincent Drill." Until 1916, the only males allowed to view the show are the firemen required by city ordinance to be on the premises. The show is replaced by the annual Gardenia Ball in 2003.

1893

The **Winthrop Building** is completed at **276–278 Washington Street**. Designed by Clarence Blackall in the Renaissance revival style, it is Boston's first entirely steel-frame skyscraper and is built on the site of the Great Spring and named for Gov. John Winthrop, whose home was nearby.

The Cyclorama Building on Tremont Street in the South End. (Courtesy of the Bostonian Society)

The **Women's New Era Club** is founded by Josephine St. Pierre Ruffin. Part of the African-American women's club movement started by Ida B. Wells, its headquarters is located at **103 Charles Street** and it lasts until 1903.

The **Boston Terrier** is first enrolled on the American Kennel Club's official stud list. The breed began sometime after 1865 with a dog named *Judge*, who was a cross between an English bulldog and a white English Terrier.

1894

The **Immigration Restriction League of Boston** is founded by "Young Brahmins" Joseph Lee, Robert DeCourcy Ward, and others. Its efforts are supported by Congressman Henry Cabot Lodge Sr., who later declares: "The lowering of a great race means not only its decline, but that of civilization."

Locke-Ober's restaurant opens at **3 Winter Place** by combining Frank Locke's wine bar (est. 1892) with Louis Ober's French restaurant (est. 1868). Famous for its Sweetbreads Eugenie and Lobster Savannah, the restaurant excludes women from the downstairs dining room (except on New Year's Eve or the evening of the Harvard-Yale football game—*if* played in Cambridge and *if* Harvard wins). That practice is ended in 1970.

June. The **New England Baptist Hospital** is founded in a house at **47 Bellevue Street** in the Longwood area. The hospital moves to the former Bond mansion on Mission Hill and builds a new hospital at **125 Parker Hill Avenue** in 1924, purchases the adjacent Robert Breck Brigham Hospital in 1969, and builds a new hospital next door to that in 1986.

1895

March 11. The **Boston Public Library** opens at **700 Boylston Street** in Copley Square. Designed by McKim, Mead & White in the Italian Renaissance style, it is

Skating on Jamaica Pond, from Ballou's Pictorial. (Courtesy of the Bostonian Society)

described by Oliver Wendell Holmes Sr. as "a palace for the people." Later known as the McKim building, it features bronze doors by Daniel Chester French, carved panels and two lions by Louis Saint-Gaudens, and staircase murals on the first and second floor by Puvis de Chavannes and Edwin Austin Abbey. John Singer Sargent's third-floor murals are installed prior to 1920. The building also contains the first children's library in the U.S. An addition, designed by Philip Johnson, opens in 1972.

The **Old Suffolk County Courthouse** is built in **Pemberton Square**. Designed by George A. Clough in the German Renaissance/French second empire style, it is re-named the John Adams Courthouse in 2002.

King Gillette invents the "safety razor" with disposable blade in an apartment at **64 Westland Avenue** in the Fenway. He joins with engineer William E. Nickerson to open the American Safety Razor Company above a fish store at **424 Atlantic Avenue** in 1901, which becomes the Gillette Safety Razor Company a year later. For many years one of the largest employers in Boston, the company is acquired by Procter & Gamble in 2005.

1896

April 6. **James Brendan Connolly** of South Boston wins the first event (the hop, step, and jump) in the first modern Olympics in Athens, Greece. A Harvard freshman, he was forced to drop out of college in order to compete.

Fannie Farmer's *Boston Cooking-School Cook Book* is published by the principal of the school, which is located at **174 Tremont Street**. The book provides the first recipes with precise measurements and introduces such local favorites as fish chowder, baked beans, and Indian pudding. Farmer founds her own cooking school at **40 Hereford Street** in 1902.

Electric trolley cars on Tremont Street, 1895. (Courtesy of the Bostonian Society, Boston Elevated Collection)

The **Massachusetts Audubon Society** is established. The oldest in the country, it is the outgrowth of efforts by Harriet Hemenway and Mina Hall to save the Snowy Egret, hunted for plumes to decorate women's hats. The organization's headquarters is initially located in Hemenway's home at **273 Clarendon Street** and today located in Lincoln.

Photographer **Walter Dodd** produces the first X-ray image taken in the U.S. at Massachusetts General Hospital on **Blossom Street** in the West End. Dodd later goes on to graduate from medical school. He returns to work at the hospital, however, and soon after contracts cancer—probably due to overexposure to the X-rays.

July. **Charles Follen McKim** attempts to donate the statue *Bacchante with Infant Faun*, by Frederick MacMonnies, to the Boston Public Library at **700 Boylston Street**. The joyfully nude figure is initially installed in the library's courtyard, but after it is denounced for its "glorification of that which is low and sensual and degrading," the library trustees ask McKim to take it back. He does—and donates it instead to New York's Metropolitan Museum of Art. A bronze replica is eventually reinstalled in the library courtyard—but not until the late 1990s.

1897

April 19. **John McDermott** wins the first **Boston Marathon** in a time of 2:55:10. It is the second marathon run in the U.S. after one run in Stamford, Connecticut, six months before, and the first to become an annual event. When it is discovered that the original course covered only 24.5 miles, the starting line is moved to Hopkinton and the distance increased to 26 miles, 385 yards in 1927. The finish line today is in front

Boston Public Library at Copley Square, ca. 1895. (Courtesy of the Bostonian Society)

of the Boston Public Library at **700 Boylston Street**. The race is originally only for amateurs; prize money is awarded beginning in 1986.

The **Franklin Park Golf Course** opens at **1 Circuit Drive** in Dorchester. Designed by Willie Campbell, the nine-hole course is the second public golf course in the country after the one in New York City's Van Cortland Park and an improvement on the unofficial, six-hole layout that had opened nearby the year before. The present Donald Ross–designed 18-hole course opens in 1923. Closed in 1975, the course is restored and reopens in the mid-1980s.

May 31. The **Robert Gould Shaw and the 54th Regiment Memorial** is dedicated across from the State House at **24 Beacon Street**. Created by sculptor Augustus Saint-Gaudens, it had initially been envisioned that only Shaw would be depicted on the frieze, but his family demanded that the troops be included as well. Despite a drenching rain, thousands turn out for the ceremony. Speakers include Booker T. Washington and William James, whose two brothers had been officers in the regiment.

The **First Corps of Cadets Armory** (today's Park Plaza "Castle") opens at **130 Columbus Avenue** in Park Square. Designed by William Preston, it is built as headquarters for volunteer militia units, which at the time were often called upon to preserve social order. The hall is today an exhibit and function hall for the Park Plaza Hotel.

September 1. The **Boston Subway** opens as an estimated 100,000 people line up to pay the 5-cent fare for the ride between today's **Park Street Station** and **Arlington Street**. It is the first major subway in the U.S. and fourth in the world after London, Budapest, and Glasgow. The line is extended to North Station in 1898, to Lechmere in 1912, and to Kenmore Square in 1914.

Construction of the Boylston Street subway station, 1896. (Courtesy of the Bostonian Society, Boston Elevated Collection)

"The Ten" is formed by a group of Boston and New York artists including Frank Benson, Joseph DeCamp, Childe Hassam, and Edmund Tarbell. Its members withdraw from the Society of American Artists and the National Academy of Design to protest the organizations' conservative tastes and large shows. The group holds smaller exhibitions of its members' works beginning a year later and continuing for the next 20 years.

1898

Robert Woods's *The City Wilderness*, a study of the South End, is published. It is considered the first social survey to be published in the U.S. Among the goals that Woods describes for settlement houses are to "reestablish on a natural basis those relations which modern city life has thrown into confusion . . . to rehabilitate neighborhood life and give it some of that healthy corporate vitality which a well-ordered village has . . . and to furnish neutral grounds where separated classes, rich and poor, professional,. and industrial, capitalist and wage-earning, may meet each other on the basis of common humanity."

October 3. **Northeastern University** is founded. Originally the Department of Law of the Boston YMCA's Evening Institute for Young Men, the first classes are held in the YMCA building at the corner of **Berkeley** and **Boylston Streets**. The school is renamed Northeastern College in 1916, then Northeastern University in 1935. It formally separates from the YMCA in 1944 and moves to its current location at **360 Huntington Avenue** in 1938.

Symphony Hall on Huntington Avenue, as shown on a postcard. (Courtesy of the Bostonian Society)

 November 26–27. The **Portland Gale** strikes Boston. It is named for the steamship *Portland,* which sinks soon after leaving Boston Harbor, drowning all 192 aboard in the worst maritime disaster in the city's history.

1899

 January 1. **South Station** opens at today's **1 South Station**. At the dedication two days before, Boston Mayor **Josiah Quincy III** declares that the new station "will raise to a distinctly higher level the impression which Boston will hereafter make upon the traveler who visits our city." Designed by Shepley, Rutan, and Coolidge in the classical revival style, it is the busiest in the world until 1913. The train shed, the largest in the world at the time, is torn down in 1930, and the wings attached to the headhouse are removed in the 1970s. Slated for demolition in 1975, the building is instead preserved, with the work completed in 1989.

 December 12. Boston dentist **Dr. George Franklin Grant** receives a patent for the golf tee. The device is meant to replace the mound of sand which players had used to elevate the ball when driving. Dr. Grant, a regular golfer at Franklin Park, is the second African-American graduate of Harvard Dental School and the first to serve on the school's faculty.

1900
Boston's population is 560,892. It is the fifth largest city in the U.S.

August 8–10. The U.S. beats Britain 3–0 in the first **Davis Cup** tennis championship, which is played at the original site of the Longwood Cricket Club on **Brookline Avenue**.

October 15. **Symphony Hall** opens at **301 Massachusetts Avenue**. Designed by Charles Follen McKim in the Italian Renaissance style, the acoustic engineering is by Harvard physics professor Wallace Clement Sabine. Originally called the new Music Hall, it comes to be regarded as one of the finest concert halls in the world. The Friday afternoon orchestra "rehearsals" soon become a Boston institution and, according to author Lucius Beebe, "assume the aspect of holy days dedicated to the classics and a vast craning of necks to be certain that the Hallowells and Forbeses are in their accustomed stalls."

December 20. **Colonial Theatre** opens at **106 Boylston Street**, with a production of *Ben Hur* that features a cast of 350 and a dozen horse-drawn chariots. The next day's *Boston Globe* declares: "Nothing so beautiful, pictorial and mechanical has ever been seen before on a Boston stage." Designed by Clarence Blackall, the 1,700-seat theater books a list of performers that would range from Fred and Adele Astaire, Fanny Brice, and Will Rogers to Laurence Olivier, Cole Porter, Paul Robeson, and Ethel Waters.

1901

March 17. The first official Evacuation Day Parade (**St. Patrick's Day Parade**) is held from City Point in South Boston to Faneuil Hall. Although a parade was held as early as 1862 and annual parades were held at least from 1876, this is the first year that the day is declared an official city holiday.

November 9. The first issue of the *Guardian* appears, founded by **William Monroe Trotter** and others. Trotter, a magna cum laud graduate of Harvard who was the first African-American elected to Phi Beta Kappa, is the publisher and advocates for a more aggressive approach to civil rights, later writing: "This is the home of abolition, of equal rights. It leads in these principles the rest of the country. Reaction is setting in. Any compromise in Boston will doubly damage the cause." After Trotter's death in 1934, his family continues to publish the newspaper until 1957.

1902

January 9. The **Aero Club of New England** is organized. The first aeronautical club in the U.S., the organization soon purchases two balloons, the *Boston* and the *Massachusetts*. Members' interest shifts to airplanes, however, after 1910.

Beth Israel Hospital is founded at **105 Chambers Street** in the West End. Originally the Mt. Sinai Dispensary, it moves to the former Dennison Estate at 59 Townsend Street in Roxbury in 1917, and to its current location at **330 Brookline Avenue** in the Longwood area in 1928, and merges with the New England Deaconess Hospital in 1996.

Robert Woods's *Americans in Process: A Settlement Study*, a study of settlement houses in the North and West Ends, is published. In it, he writes: "There are actually streets in the West End where, while Jews are moving in, Negro housewives are gathering up their skirts and seeking a more spotless environment."

1903

January 1. **Isabella Stewart Gardner's Fenway Court** opens at **280 The Fenway**. Guests, including William James and Edith Wharton, are served champagne and doughnuts. Although the building is officially designed by William T. Sears, Mrs. Gardner was involved with every detail of the design, construction, and decoration of the Venetian-style *palazzo*. Henry Adams later describes the building and garden as "peace, repose or dream, rather like opium." After Mrs. Gardner's death, the building reopens as a museum in 1925.

February 16. The **Majestic Theatre** opens at **219 Tremont Street**, with a performance of the "musical fantasy" *The Storks*. Designed by John Galen Howard in the Beaux-Arts style for Eben Jordan, the 1,700-seat theater houses opera, theater, and vaudeville. Later transformed to the Saxon movie house, it is purchased by Emerson College and restored, and reopens as the Cutler Majestic in 2003.

February. The **Good Government Association** (GGA, or "Goo-Goos") is established. Created by the Chamber of Commerce, the Massachusetts Bar Association, the Merchants Association, the Associated Board of Trade, and the Fruit and Produce Association, its goal is to reduce corruption and inefficiency in government and support candidates of talent and integrity for elective office. The organization includes individuals like Louis D. Brandeis, Edward A. Filene, and Robert A. Woods.

July 30. The **"Boston Riot"** occurs at the Columbus Avenue A.M.E. Zion Church at **600 Columbus Avenue**, when William Monroe Trotter and others interrupt a talk by Booker T. Washington. The demonstrators are critical of what they believe is Washington's "accommodationist" approach to civil rights. Police are called and several people are arrested, including Trotter, who spends a month in the Charles Street Jail at **215 Charles Street**.

September 24. **James Michael Curley** and Thomas Curley (no relation) are convicted of having taken a postal service exam for two Irish immigrants on December 4, 1902. They are sentenced to serve 60 days in the Charles Street Jail at **215 Charles Street**. Despite his conviction and incarceration, Curley wins election to the Board of Aldermen, running on the slogan: "I did it for a friend."

October 13. The Boston American League team beats the Pittsburg (sic) Pirates of the

*First Church
of Christ, Scientist,
on Massachusetts
Avenue, ca. 1906.*
(Courtesy of the
Bostonian Society)

National League 3–0 in game 8 at the Huntington Avenue Grounds at **400 Huntington Avenue** to win the first-ever World Series. The team was founded in 1901, is sometimes called the Americans or the Pilgrims, and does not become the Red Sox until 1907.

October 20. **Jordan Hall** opens at **30 Gainsborough Street** with a performance of George Whitefield Chadwick's *Melpomene* by the Boston Symphony Orchestra. Designed by Wheelwright and Haven with acoustics by Wallace Clement Sabine, the 1,019-seat hall is a gift from Eben Jordan to the New England Conservatory of Music.

November 14. **Harvard loses to Dartmouth** 11–0 in the first football game played at **Harvard Stadium** at **95 North Harvard Street**. Designed by in McKim, Mead & White, it is the world's first massive, reinforced-concrete building and the country's first large collegiate stadium. Its initial seating capacity of 22,000 is later increased to as much as 58,000, and is currently 37,000.

1904

November 11. A fire at the **Harcourt Building** on **Harcourt Street** destroys the life's work of many of Boston's most accomplished artists, including William Worcester Churchill, Joseph DeCamp, Mary Brewster Hazleton, William Paxton, Elizabeth Vila Taylor (later Watson), and Theodore Wendel. On the day after the fire, DeCamp reportedly walks into the St. Botolph Club, then at **2 Newbury Street**, and announces "I have a family to support. I'll paint anybody's portrait for $100."

1905

November 21. The **Fenway Studios** open at **30 Ipswich Street**. Designed by Parker and Thomas in the arts & crafts/Beaux-Arts style, it becomes the home of some of Boston's foremost artists. According to the *Boston Sunday Globe*: "Late suppers and noisy revelers, associated from long since with studio life, are here rare. It is a

The Museum of Fine Arts on Huntington Avenue, as shown on a postcard. (Courtesy of the Bostonian Society)

Boston atmosphere that one finds in the building, of respectability and quiet, yet an atmosphere of art withal."

December 12. Democrat **John F. Fitzgerald** is elected the first American-born, Irish-Catholic mayor of Boston. One of seven children, Fitzgerald is a graduate of Boston Latin School who was forced to withdraw from Harvard Medical School after the deaths of his mother and father. A former state senator and U.S. congressman, he promises "a bigger, better, busier Boston."

1906

H.G. Wells visits Boston and leaves less than impressed. In *The Future America,* he later writes: "Boston presents a terrible, terrifying unanimity of aesthetic discriminations. There broods over the real Boston an immense sense of finality. One feels in Boston, as one feels in no other part of the States, that the intellectual movement has ceased. . . . The capacity of Boston, it would seem, was just sufficient but no more than sufficient, to comprehend the whole achievement of the human intellect up, let us say, to the year 1875. Then an equilibrium was established. At or about that year Boston filled up."

1907

The Education of Henry Adams is first published, privately by the author in a very limited edition. Among its descriptions of Boston is this one: "Boston had solved the universe; or had offered and realized the best solution yet tried. The problem was worked out."

July. The **Boston Finance Commission** (FinCom) is created by the Republican-dominated legislature to scrutinize the financial practices of the Democratic-dominated city government. The commission proceeds to hold a number of hearings and issues a scathing four-volume report, which includes the charge that "administrative offices are given out as a reward for party work; and the number and the salaries are increased beyond the requirements of the service." The FinCom continues to analyze city finances today.

 Albert Champion, a former French bicycle racer, invents the AC spark plug in his shop in the Cyclorama Building at **539 Tremont Street** in the South End.

1908

 January 29. **William Henry O'Connell** is installed Catholic archbishop of Boston. Nicknamed "Gangplank Bill" for his frequent sea cruises and "Number One" for his influence. O'Connell presides over a weeklong centennial of the founding of the archdiocese beginning on October 28. There, he declares: "The Puritan has passed, the Catholic remains. The city where a century ago, he came unwanted, he has made his own. . . It is time for Catholic manhood to stand erect, square its shoulders, look the world in the eye and say, "I am a Roman Catholic citizen; What about it?"

 February 23. The **Ford Hall Forum** holds its first lecture at Ford Hall on **Ashburton Place** on Beacon Hill. The oldest, continually held lecture series in the U.S., it is founded by businessman George Coleman and sponsored by the Boston Baptist Social Union to provide "moral and intellectual stimulus, without prejudice to race, creed or class." Speakers would include Winston Churchill, Clarence Darrow, W.E.B. Du Bois, Alexander Kerensky, Dr. Martin Luther King Jr., Henry Kissinger, Norman Mailer, Reinhold Niebuhr, Ayn Rand, Elie Wiesel, and Malcolm X. The lectures continue today in various venues around the city.

1909

 March 30. The **"New Boston 1915"** campaign is launched by Edward Filene, Louis D. Brandeis, James Jackson Storrow, Robert Woods, and others to develop a comprehensive physical and social plan for the Boston area. But the organization dissolves soon after its bill to establish a metropolitan government is defeated in the Massachusetts legislature in 1912.

 The first **Joe & Nemo's** opens in Scollay Square. Originally a hot dog stand operated by Joseph Merlino and Anthony Calogerre, it becomes a restaurant on **Howard Street** in 1936. The Scollay Square restaurant closes in June 1963, and all of the Boston restaurants close by 1984.

 November 15. The current **Museum of Fine Arts** opens at **465 Huntington Avenue** in the Fenway. Founded in 1870, the museum initially operated on the top floor of the Boston Athenaeum before moving to Copley Square in 1876. The new building is designed by Guy Lowell and features murals by John Singer Sargent. The Evans Wing opens in 1915, the Decorative Arts Wing in 1928, the George Robert White Wing in 1970, the West Wing in 1981, and the American Wing in 2010.

1910

 January 11. Democrat **John F. Fitzgerald** narrowly defeats Republican **James Jackson**

C. Grahame-White at the Harvard-Boston Aero Meet, 1910. (Courtesy of the Bostonian Society)

Storrow in one of the closest elections in city history to become mayor of Boston, the first to serve a four-year term. The election pitted the emerging Irish-Catholic majority against the waning Yankee Protestant establishment. During the campaign, Storrow equated "Fitzgeraldism" with corruption, while Fitzgerald campaigned on the slogan "Manhood against Money."

June 30. The **Charles River Dam** is completed. Construction of the dam alleviates the sanitation problems at low tide that the Board of Health had described as "an atmosphere of stench so strong as to arouse the sleeping, terrify the weak, and nauseate and exasperate nearly everybody . . . It visits the rich and poor alike." It also allows for construction of the Esplanade along the banks of the river. A new dam is completed behind North Station on the site of the former Warren Street Bridge in 1978.

Dr. John Collins Bossidy writes an ode to Boston that is delivered as a toast at a Holy Cross reunion held at Harvard University: "And this is dear old Boston,/The home of the bean and the cod,/Where the Lowells talk only to the Cabots,/And the Cabots talk only to God."

The first annual Feast of the Madonna del Soccorso is held in the **North End**. The oldest of the neighborhood's so-called "**Fishermen's Feasts**," it would be followed by the Feasts of St. Agrippina di Mineo, St. Anthony, St. Dominic, St. Joseph, St. Jude, St. Lucia, St. Rocco, St. Rosallia, Madonna del Grazie, and Madonna Della Cava.
The **Chilton Club** is organized. Named for Mary Chilton, the only passenger on the Mayflower to move from Plymouth to Boston, it is the first female counterpart to the city's many exclusive men's clubs. Soon after its founding, the club acquires its headquarters at **287 Dartmouth Street**, a building that is reported to have three entrances—one for members only, one for members with guests, and one in the alley for servants.

December. The **Boston Arena** opens on **St. Botolph Street**. The oldest artificial-ice ice arena in the U.S., it is home to the Boston Bruins, Boston Celtics, and numerous college and high school hockey teams. Speakers at nonsporting events here would include Presidents Coolidge, Hoover, and Franklin Roosevelt, Gov. Al Smith; and Charles Lindbergh. Purchased by Northeastern University in 1977, it is renovated and reopened as Matthews Arena in 1982.

1911

July 4. The temperature reaches 104 degrees, the hottest ever recorded in Boston.

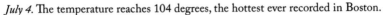

Harriet Quimby of Boston becomes the first woman in the U.S. to obtain an airplane pilot's license. Dubbed the "Dresden China Aviatrix" by the press, she becomes the first woman to fly solo across the English Channel on April 16, 1912. But on July 1, she and her passenger, William Willard, die after being thrown out of their monoplane and plunging 1,000 feet into **Dorchester Bay** during the Harvard-Boston Aero Meet. Five thousand spectators witness the accident and watch the empty plane glide down into the water with barely any damage to its fuselage.

1912

April 20. The Red Sox beat the New York Highlanders 7–6 in 11 innings before 27,000 spectators in the first official game played at **Fenway Park**. Designed by James McLaughlin, John Updike later writes of the park: "It was built in 1912 and rebuilt in 1934, and offers, as do most Boston artifacts, a compromise between Man's Euclidean determinations and Nature's beguiling irregularities." The team goes on to beat the New York Giants to win the World Series in 1912. The Red Sox also win the World Series in 1915, 1916, and 1918 against the Philadelphia Phillies, Brooklyn Robins and Chicago Cubs, respectively.

The **Boston Branch of the National Association for the Advancement of Colored People** (NAACP) is founded at Park Street Church at **1 Park Street**. It is the first official branch of the organization in the U.S. A white man, Moorfield Storey, is the first president. Butler Wilson becomes the first African-American president in 1926.

The **Fairmont Copley Plaza Hotel** opens at **138 St. James Avenue** in Copley Square. Designed by Blackall and Hardenbergh in the Italian Renaissance style, it later includes the revolving Merry-Go-Round Lounge, which operated from 1933 until it was dismantled in the 1970s.

$ *September 3.* Over 200,000 people gather for the opening of the new **Filene's** department store building at **426 Washington Street**. Designed by Daniel Burnham in the Beaux-Arts style, the building houses both the upstairs store (est. 1881) and **Filene's Basement** (est. 1908). The basement store institutes its "automatic markdown" policy in 1911 and later becomes a separate company. Filene's is later acquired by May Department Stores and closes in 2007.

December. The first municipal **Christmas tree lighting** is held on **Boston Common**. Ten thousand people join Boston Mayor **John F. Fitzgerald** in the lighting of the 35-foot tree. According to his biographer, Fitzgerald instituted the practice after hearing a derelict on **Boston Common** complain the year before: "This is Christmas Eve, but there is no Christmas for me." New York, Chicago, Philadelphia, and Washington subsequently follow Boston's example and establish their own ceremonies.

1913

January 27. **Peter Bent Brigham Hospital** is founded on the site of the former Francis estate in the Fenway. The hospital was endowed by and named for a Boston restaurant owner and real estate mogul who died in 1877. It merges with other hospitals to form Brigham and Women's Hospital in 1980.

Commonwealth Pier opens. The largest pier on the East Coast at the time, it is built by the state to accommodate large ocean liners. It is later renovated into a meeting and convention facility and renamed the World Trade Center in 1986.

The **Franklin Park Zoo** opens at today's **1 Franklin Park Road**. Annual attendance reaches 1 million visitors in the 1930s and 1940s. Operated initially by the city, it is today operated by Zoo New England.

The **Children's Museum** opens in Jamaica Plain. The second oldest children's museum in the U.S. after one in Brooklyn, which opened in 1899, it moves to Pinebank in the 1920s, to the former Morse/Milton estate on Burroughs Street in March 1936, and to its current location on Museum Wharf at **300 Congress Street** in 1979.

August 4. The *Boston Post* conducts its most outlandish promotion when it sends **Joseph Knowles**, a 44-year-old illustrator at the paper, into the woods of northern Maine for 60 days. Knowles is supposedly naked, unarmed, and without food or water. He is not allowed to have contact with another human being and is supposed to survive on his own wiles—living on roots, berries, and game he somehow manages to catch—and file stories and drawings describing his experience by making charcoal markings on birch bark that he leaves at a designated location. After he emerges from the woods across the border in Canada two months later, Knowles is taken by private train to Boston where he is met by a crowd of as many as 400,000 people on Newspaper Row, eager to see this "survivor." Despite later reports of the discovery of a campground containing a fire pit and empty food cans near where Knowles first entered the woods, he is later called upon to repeat his feat by a Hearst newspaper in California.

1914

January 13. **James Michael Curley** is elected mayor of Boston for the first of four terms he would serve in four different decades. Curley would be called "Mayor of the Poor" and initiate numerous job-producing public works projects that led to the construction of roads, bridges, beaches, municipal buildings, neighborhood health clinics, and a rebuilt Boston City Hospital. An outstanding if florid orator, he would also become known for antagonizing, the Yankee business establishment, ignoring ward bosses, and, as Thomas O'Connor later writes "claiming the people as his only

constituency."

February 21. In an article in the *Boston Globe,* Lincoln Steffens states: "Boston is the case of a failure of government by good people. Boston is paved with good intentions. So is Hell ... Boston is a common city of superior people. It has all the good things that other cities think, if they had them, would make impossible political corruption. Yet Boston has always had the good things and has always had political corruption."

October 7. **Rose Fitzgerald**, the daughter of former Boston Mayor John F. Fitzgerald, marries **Joseph P. Kennedy**, the son of East Boston ward boss P. J. Kennedy, in a wedding officiated by Cardinal O'Connell in the cardinal's private chapel at **2102 Commonwealth Avenue** in Brighton. Their children would constitute one of the most famous, effective, and tragic political dynasties in U.S. history.

The Custom House tower after its completion, 1916. (Courtesy of the Bostonian Society)

October 13. The Boston Braves beat the Philadelphia Athletics 3–1 in game 4 to win their only World Series in Boston. The team is called the "**Miracle Braves**" because its wins the pennant after being in last place on July 19. Because the team's new stadium, Braves Field on **Commonwealth Avenue**, is under construction, the Braves play games 3 and 4 of the World Series at **Fenway Park**. The team leaves Boston—first for Milwaukee and then for Atlanta—in 1952.

1915

January 18. The **Custom House Tower** opens at **3 McKinley Square**. The 32-story, 496-foot tower designed by Peabody & Stearns added to the original building makes it the tallest in Boston, a distinction that would last until 1947. Its construction is allowed only because federally owned buildings are not subject to the city's 125-foot height limit. The federal government declares the building surplus in 1986 and the building is converted into time-share condominiums in 1997.

April 17. Despite protests led by William Monroe Trotter, D.W. Griffith's film *The Birth of a Nation* opens at the Tremont Theatre at **176 Tremont Street**. Based on Thomas Dixon's play *The Clansman*, it portrays slaves as savages and glorifies the Ku Klux Klan. The film is screened for the next 6½ months, but Trotter and others eventually persuade city officials to bar a proposed return engagement in 1921.

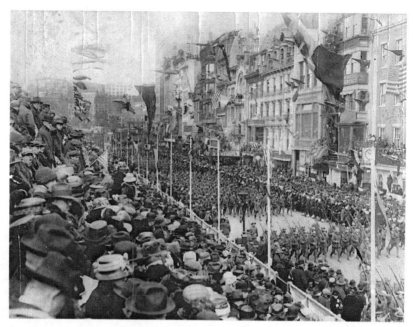

A parade down Tremont Street for returning Word War I soldiers. (Courtesy of the Bostonian Society)

November 11. **Roland Hayes** makes his Boston singing debut in Jordan Hall at **30 Gainsborough Street**. After moving o Boston to study in 1911, Hayes spends—and loses—his life savings of $200 to produce the concert. Later one of the first African-American singers to perform with major symphony orchestras and tour internationally, he first performs at Symphony Hall on November 15, 1917, and continues to perform until 1972.

1916

January 28. **Louis D. Brandeis** is nominated to the U.S. Supreme Court by President Wilson. A graduate of Harvard Law School who became very active in civic affairs in Boston, he becomes the first Jew on the nation's highest court when he is confirmed on June 1 and sworn in on June 5.

November 12. Evangelist **Billy Sunday** preaches to an estimated 55,000 people (another 15,000 are turned away) in a tabernacle erected on **Huntington Avenue**. A former major league baseball player, Sunday calls himself "the Lord's third base coach—trying to get the sinners home." His 10-week crusade in Boston attracts an estimated 1.5 million people.

1917

February 13. **"Rat Day"** is held. Sponsored by the Boston Women's Municipal League to encourage the depletion of the city's rodent population, prizes are awarded to citizens who bring in the most dead rats.

Blinstrub's Village is opened at **308 West Broadway** in South Boston by Stanley

Blinstrub. The original restaurant is expanded into a nightclub with 1,700 seats, making it one of the largest in the country. Entertainers performing here would include Ray Charles, Nat King Cole, Sammy Davis Jr., Jimmy Durante, Wayne Newton, and Patti Page. The nightclub is destroyed by a fire on February 7, 1968.

1918

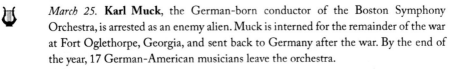

March 25. **Karl Muck**, the German-born conductor of the Boston Symphony Orchestra, is arrested as an enemy alien. Muck is interned for the remainder of the war at Fort Oglethorpe, Georgia, and sent back to Germany after the war. By the end of the year, 17 German-American musicians leave the orchestra.

August 27. Two sailors on board the Receiving Ship at **Commonwealth Pier** report to sick bay. Three days later, over 60 are diagnosed with **Spanish Influenza**. On September 3, the first civilian flu casualties are admitted to Boston City Hospital. Between September and December, the flu claims nearly 4,800 victims in Boston.

November 11. The **Strand Theatre** opens at **543 Columbia Road** in Dorchester. Designed by Funk and Wilcox, it is later described as "Boston's first great movie palace." The theater also hosts live entertainment. Performers who appear at the 1,400-seat theater would include Fred Allen, Jack Benny, Fanny Brice, Milton Berle, Tommy Dorsey, and Ray Bolger. The building is taken over by the city in 1975 and reopens as the M. Harriet McCormack Center for the Arts in 1979.

1919

January 15. The **Great Molasses Flood** occurs when a 50-foot-high, 90-foot-diameter tank owned by the Purity Distilling Company at **529 Commercial Street** in the North End collapses, releasing a 15-foot-high wave containing over 2 million gallons of molasses. Twenty-one people are killed and more than 150 injured. The *Boston Post* reports that: "horses were blown about like chips, houses torn asunder, and the heavy section of the Elevated railroad structure smashed like an eggshell." Although "anarchists" are initially suspected of sabotage (the molasses was to be used in the production of munitions), the cause is later attributed to shoddy construction of the tank and the rapid expansion of the molasses due to unusually warm weather.

August. Boston bookmaker **Joe "Sport" Sullivan** and Chicago White Sox first baseman **Chick Gandil** meet at the Hotel Buckminster at **645 Beacon Street** in Kenmore Square and plan to fix the upcoming World Series, which leads to the famous "**Black Sox Scandal.**"

September 9. The **Boston Police Strike** takes place when over 1,100 of the city's 1,500 officers walk off the job. One of several labor strikes in the city this year, it is held to protest low salaries and the administration's refusal to allow police officers to form a union. Three days of rioting and looting follow in which nine people are killed and 23 wounded. Massachusetts Governor **Calvin Coolidge** calls out the state National Guard and declares: "There is no right to strike against the public safety by anybody, anywhere, anytime." Order is eventually restored and, although the demands of the

THE BOSTON POST
HUGE MOLASSES TANK EXPLODES IN NORTH END; 11 DEAD, 50 HURT

Giant Wave of 2,300,000 Gallons of Molasses, 50 Feet High, Sweeps Everything Before It—100 Men Women and Children Caught in Sticky Stream—Buildings, Vehicles and L Structure Crushed

35 STATES ON DRY LAW LIST

Amendment Ratfied by Five Yesterday—One More Needed—Predict Nation Dry July 1

SECRECY IN PEACE

Search for More Victims During the Night
No Escape From Gigantic Wave of Fluid

INTERNAL EXPLOSION WAS CAUSE, SAYS STATE CHEMIST

The Boston Post headline following the Molasses Flood, 1919. (Courtesy of the Bostonian Society)

police officers are later met, none of the strikers is ever be rehired.

1920

January 5. The Red Sox announce the sale of **Babe Ruth** to New York Yankees for $125,000 and a $300,000 loan to Red Sox owner and Broadway producer **Harry Frazee**. The transaction sparks outrage in Boston, with one newspaper featuring cartoons of Faneuil Hall and the Boston Public Library with "For Sale" signs on them. Ruth is not the only Red Sox player sold or traded to the Yankees; two years later, New York wins the World Series with 11 former Red Sox players.

The **East Boston Immigration Station** opens at **287 Marginal Street** in East Boston. Although the building includes a cafeteria, dormitories for men and women, and a roof garden for exercise, it is much smaller in scale than Ellis Island because, unlike New York, Boston employs inspectors who process almost all immigrants while still aboard docked ships. The station is closed in 1954 and the building is demolished in 2011.

July 24. The *Boston Post* begins a series of stories that exposes the pyramid scheme operated by **Charles Ponzi**. An Italian immigrant, Ponzi operated from an office at **27 School Street,** where he promised investors huge returns and attracted an estimated $15 million in just over six months. Ponzi is arrested, pleads guilty on November 30, and is sent to prison. He dies in a hospital for paupers in Rio de Janeiro in 1949.

1921

When Harvard University segregates the living quarters of its five African-American freshmen from the rest of the incoming class, alumni William Monroe Trotter, W.E.B. Du Bois and others protest. Du Bois subsequently writes that the time had come "when the grandson of a slave has to teach democracy to a president of Harvard."

Members of the Boston Police Department with confiscated alcohol during Prohibition.
(Courtesy of the Bostonian Society)

September 19. Radio station **WBZ** is granted the first radio station license in Boston. The station makes its first broadcast, a live one, from the Eastern States Exposition in Springfield on September 19. WBZA, an affiliated station, begins broadcasting from a studio at the Hotel Brunswick at the corner of **Boylston** and **Clarendon Streets** in 1924, then switches call letters with the Springfield station in March 1931.

December 13. **James Michael Curley** is elected to his second term as mayor of Boston. The *Boston Herald* describes Curley as winning "without the assistance of a single political leader of either party, and with every machine of recognized standing against him." He is inaugurated in January before a crowd of 12,000 people at Mechanics Hall at **135 Huntington Avenue**.

1922

June 1. Newspapers report that, with 21% of the incoming freshman class at Harvard made up of Jewish students, Harvard president A. Lawrence Lowell has called for imposing a quota on the number of Jewish students admitted in the future. The Harvard Board of Overseers votes against excluding students on the basis of race or ethnic background in April 1923.

November 7. **Susan Walker Fitzgerald** becomes the first woman Democrat in the Massachusetts legislature when she is elected state representative from Jamaica Plain. **M. Sylvia Donaldson** becomes the first woman Republican when she is elected state representative from Brockton in the same election.

1923

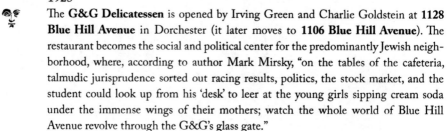

The **G&G Delicatessen** is opened by Irving Green and Charlie Goldstein at **1128 Blue Hill Avenue** in Dorchester (it later moves to **1106 Blue Hill Avenue**). The restaurant becomes the social and political center for the predominantly Jewish neighborhood, where, according to author **Mark Mirsky**, "on the tables of the cafeteria, talmudic jurisprudence sorted out racing results, politics, the stock market, and the student could look up from his 'desk' to leer at the young girls sipping cream soda under the immense wings of their mothers; watch the whole world of Blue Hill Avenue revolve through the G&G's glass gate."

The psychic "**Margery**" begins holding seances in her home at **10 Lime Street** on Beacon Hill. The Canadian-born wife of Dr. Le Roi Goddard Crandon, a lecturer at Harvard Medical School, Mrs. Crandon's psychic powers are consulted by fashionable Bostonians, investigated by *Scientific American* magazine, and doubted by Harry Houdini.

September 8. **Logan Airport** is dedicated on what had been tidal flats at Jeffries Point in East Boston. Built and operated by the U.S. Army, the first regular passenger service to New York begins in 1927. The army transfers ownership to the state in 1928, which leases it to the city of Boston in 1929, then resumes control in 1941. Originally called Boston Airport, it is renamed Commonwealth Airport in 1944, then named for Maj. Gen. Edward L. Logan, a South Boston native and commander of the Yankee Division —despite the fact that Logan had never flown in an airplane. The Massachusetts Port Authority assumes operation of the airport in 1959.

1924

March 21. Boston stockbroker L. Sherman Adams introduces the Massachusetts Investors Trust at the Boston Stock Exchange. The first mutual fund—as it comes to be called—it is initially called a "**Boston fund.**" Adams's company is today called MFS Investment Management.

Serge Koussevitzky is named conductor of the Boston Symphony Orchestra. Considered one of the great figures in 20th-century music—as a musician, conductor, composer, music publisher, teacher, and promoter of new music and musicians' rights—he is named to the newly created post of music director in 1947 and continues to lead the orchestra until 1949.

December 24. The first annual **Beacon Hill Christmas Eve Bell Ringing** is held in Louisburg Square. The practice is initiated by Mrs. Arthur Shurcliff, the former Margaret Nichols. The bell ringing has continued every year to this day—except for one year during World War II when a blackout was imposed.

1925

July 4. Shortly before 3 a.m., the **Dreyfus Hotel** collapses at **12 Beach Street**, killing 44 people. The building had been damaged by a fire 10 weeks earlier, but the collapse itself is attributed to dancers doing the Charleston in the second-floor Pickwick Club and shaking the building.

October 16. The **Metropolitan Theatre** opens at **270 Tremont Street**. Designed by Clarence Blackall as a "movie palace," it is New England's largest theater with more than 3,800 seats. An estimated at 20,000 people attend the public opening a night later, and the *Boston Advertiser* describes them "rubbing their eyes and wondering if it was all a dream." The theater is later renamed the Music Hall, then the Wang Center for the Performing Arts, and is today called the Citi Performing Arts Center.

November 3. **Malcolm E. Nichols** becomes the last Republican to be elected mayor of Boston to date. Nichols is the former regional head of the Internal Revenue Service. His administration, ironically, would be criticized for allowing corruption.

November 10. The **Huntington Theatre** opens at **264 Huntington Avenue**. Designed by J. William Beal & Sons, the Georgian revival-style building is originally called the Repertory Theatre and is home to a short-lived professional repertory company. It later becomes Civic Repertory Theatre, featuring out-of-work actors as part of the federal WPA project, and is today owned by Boston University.

December. In an article entitled **"Boston Twilight"** in the December issue of the *American Mercury*, Charles Angoff declares: "Boston culture has collapsed...In literature, where it once held hegemony, it is now a Sahara; theatrically it is the paradise of the cheapest leg shows; musically it is sinking daily... Outside of servants, traffic cops and low politicians the Irish Catholics have given Boston nothing. Perhaps the old Boston culture was doomed to collapse anyhow. But one thing is certain: the invasion of these barbarians made its further growth impossible, and its renaissance will not take place until they are exterminated."

1926

April 5. **H.L. Mencken** is arrested on **Boston Common** when he sells a copy of his *American Mercury* magazine to **J. Franklin Chase**, secretary of the Watch and Ward Society. Mencken is charged with purveying obscenity because the magazine contains a short story which describes the life of a prostitute. The charge is dropped in court the next day and Mencken celebrates by going to lunch at the Harvard Club with Professor Zachariah Chafee and Felix Frankfurter. But the Watch and Ward Society later persuades the U.S. Post Office to bar the magazine from being sent by mail to its subscribers.

Regina Pizza is founded by Italian immigrant Anthony Polcari at **11½ Thatcher Street** in the North End. Long reputed for serving the best pizza in Boston, the original restaurant continues to operate along with more than 15 others in and around Boston.

1927

January 28. **Aaron Copland**'s *Concerto for Piano (In One Movement)* is given its world premiere by the Boston Symphony Orchestra, Serge Koussevitzky conducting, at Symphony Hall. Boston music critics call it "insulting" and a "shocking lack of taste" (*Herald*), "concatenation of meaninglessly ugly sounds" (*Post*), and a "harrowing horror from beginning to end"(*Transcript*).

May 18. The **Ritz-Carlton Hotel** opens at **15 Arlington Street** in the Back Bay. It is owned and operated by Edward Wyner, who must approve all guests. Some of those guests would include Winston Churchill, Charles Lindbergh, and actor Eddie "Rochester" Anderson, who is welcomed by Wyner in 1941 when most major hotels refused to accept African-Americans as guests.

August 23. **Nicola Sacco** and **Bartolomeo Vanzetti** are executed at **Charlestown State Prison**. Italian immigrants and self-professed anarchists, they had been convicted of two murders during a payroll robbery of a Braintree shoe factory in 1920 after what many say was an unfair trial. The funeral for the two men on August 28 begins at the Langone Funeral Home at **383 Hanover Street** in the North End. More than 50,000 people begin the march to the Forest Hills Cemetery, while 200,000 people line the route, standing in the rain. The bodies of the two men are cremated. Their ashes are today stored in a locked vault in the Boston Public Library.

1928

November 14. **North Station** is dedicated on **Causeway Street**. President Calvin Coolidge throws a switch in the White House to turn on the lights in the station via telegraph. The station is replaced by a new, underground station in 1995.

November 17. **Boston Garden** opens, above the new North Station on **Causeway Street**. Built by promoter George Lewis "Tex" Rickard, the first event is a benefit boxing match in which local featherweight Dick "Honey Boy" Finnegan beats welterweight champion Andre Routis in a nontitle bout. Boston Garden is replaced by a new arena, now called the **TD Garden**, in 1995.

1929

The **Napoleon Club** opens at **52 Piedmont Street** in Bay Village. Boston's most popular gay nightclub of the era, it closes in 1998 and the building is later turned into luxury condominiums.

July 4. **Boston Sinfonietta**, Arthur Fiedler conducting, performs a free, open-air concert in a newly built wooden "shell" on today's **Esplanade**. Fiedler becomes conductor of the Boston Pops a year later, and that orchestra makes the summer outdoor concerts an annual Boston tradition that continues today.
September 30. Eugene O'Neill's play *Strange Interlude* is banned from being performed at the **Hollis Street Theatre** by Boston Mayor **Malcolm E. Nichols**, who had seen the play in New York. It is subsequently performed in Quincy and attended by that city's Mayor McGrath.

March 29. The **Boston Bruins** beat the Rangers 2–0 at Madison Square Garden to win the team's first Stanley Cup. The team was founded in 1924 and was the first U.S. team in the National Hockey League. The Bruins also win Stanley Cups in 1939 and

1949, against the Toronto Maple Leafs and Detroit Red Wings, respectively.

1930

February 19. The **United Shoe Machine Building** opens at **160 Federal Street**. Designed by Parker, Thomas and Rice in the art deco style, it is the first building to conform to the 1928 "pyramid" amendment to the city's zoning code, which allows buildings to exceed the height limits provided their upper floors "step back" from the street. It is renovated and renamed the Landmark in 1987.

September 14–20. "**Boston Week**" caps a summer-long celebration of the city's Tercentenary. Events include a 10,000-person "town meeting" in the Public Garden and an eight-hour parade featuring 40,000 marchers, 108 units, and 200 floats, watched by an estimated 1 million people. At Faneuil Hall, Boston Mayor James Michael Curley places a letter in a time capsule to be opened in 1980 in which he expresses the hope "that the career of the Mayor of 1980 would not be as tempestuous as his."

Nicola Sacco and Bartolomeo Vanzetti.
(Courtesy of the Boston Herald)

1931

January 27. An exhibit by painter "**Pavel Jerdanowitch**" is held at the Vose Galleries at **559 Boylston Street**. Although the "art" had previously won critical acclaim in New York, Chicago, and Paris, the show is later revealed to be a hoax, perpetrated by artist Paul Jordan Smith and abetted by gallery owner Robert Vose. The *Boston Post* lauds them for "introducing this element of humor" into the art world, but Charles Hovey Pepper, a member of the Boston Five group of modernist painters, decries the "cheap attempt to discredit the modernist movement."

1932

February 25. The **Paramount Theatre** opens at **539 Washington Street**. Designed by Arthur Bowditch in the art moderne style, it is one of the first in Boston to be built expressly for alking pictures. The theater closes in 1976, is later purchased by Emerson College, and reopens as a smaller live-performance theater with an adjacent "black box theater" in 2010.

July 1. Denied a place in the Massachusetts democratic delegation that supports Al Smith for president, Boston Mayor **James Michael Curley** somehow manages to be named acting chairman of the delegation from Puerto Rico. Introduced as "Alcalde

A concert at the Hatch Shell, 1943. (Courtesy of the Bostonian Society)

Jaime Miguel Curleo," he casts the delegation's votes for his candidate, Franklin Delano Roosevelt, at the Democratic National Convention in Chicago.

March 23. The **Boston Municipal Research Bureau** is established "to study Boston's fiscal, management, and administrative problems." At the organization's 60th anniversary in May 1992, current president Sam Tyler describes the "love-hate relationship" between the bureau and the city: "They love us when we say nice things, they hate us when we're critical."

1933

January 18. The **Old Howard Theatre** at **34 Howard Street** is closed down for 30 days after complaints by the Watch and Ward Society of "voluptuous dancing and profane language." It subsequently reopens with a production entitled *Scrambled Legs*. "I was continually badgered by the eager, lip-pursing members of the New England Watch and Ward Society," Boston Mayor James Michael Curley later writes, "who combined the fervor of bird-feeders and disciples of the Anti-Vivisection Society." He also declares: "the Old Howard is known in every port of the world. It is one of Boston's great institutions."

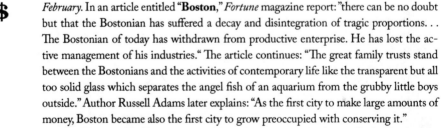

February. In an article entitled "**Boston,**" *Fortune* magazine report: "there can be no doubt but that the Bostonian has suffered a decay and disintegration of tragic proportions. . . The Bostonian of today has withdrawn from productive enterprise. He has lost the active management of his industries." The article continues: "The great family trusts stand between the Bostonians and the activities of contemporary life like the transparent but all too solid glass which separates the angel fish of an aquarium from the grubby little boys outside." Author Russell Adams later explains: "As the first city to make large amounts of money, Boston became also the first city to grow preoccupied with conserving it."

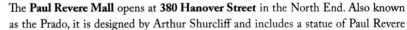

The **Paul Revere Mall** opens at **380 Hanover Street** in the North End. Also known as the Prado, it is designed by Arthur Shurcliff and includes a statue of Paul Revere

Mayor James Michael Curley throws out the first pitch at Fenway Park. (Photograph courtesy of the Boston Public Library, Print Department)

on horseback by Cyrus Dallin that was dedicated in 1940. Before the installation, a controversy arose over which church (St. Stephen's Catholic Church or Episcopal Old North Church) would be "favored" with the statue. Boston Mayor James Michael Curley decides in favor of St. Stephen's.

1934

Elliot Norton begins reviewing plays for the *Boston Post*. One of the most influential theater critics in the country, Norton soon moves to the *Record-American* (later the *Herald American*) and becomes known for assisting in "play doctoring" (making suggestions to improve plays making their pre-Broadway runs in Boston). Awarded a Tony award for his lifetime contributions to theater in 1970, Norton retires—and the first annual Elliot Norton Awards for excellence in Boston local theater begin to be awarded—in 1982.

1935

The **Mapparium** opens in the Christian Science Library building at **200 Massachusetts Avenue**. Designed by Chester Lindsay Churchill, the stained-glass globe is 30 feet in diameter and allows a view from "inside" the earth. The names of the countries represented on the globe have not been changed since it opened this year.

Simco's on the Bridge opens at **1509 Blue Hill Avenue** in Mattapan. Noted for its foot-long hot dogs, the restaurant is a popular after-prom destination for local high school students. It is destroyed by a fire in 1989 and reopens two years later under a new name—Simco's by the Bridge.

July 10. **Suffolk Downs Raceway** opens at **111 Waldemar Avenue** in East Boston, as 35,000 fans watch Eddie Wrack, ridden by Carl Hanford, win the first race. Designed

by Mark Linenthal, the track is built for Thoroughbred horse racing and continues in operation today.

1936

The **Charles River Embankment** (later the Storrow Memorial Embankment and today known as the **Esplanade**) is dedicated. Although a commission had recommended that a highway be constructed as part of the enlarged riverside park, the proposal was dropped when **Helen Osbourne Storrow**, the widow of **James Jackson Storrow** and a $1 million contributor to the project, objected. After her death in 1944, the proposal to construct the highway is revived and the Esplanade is widened in 1950. The highway, named **Storrow Drive**, is completed in 1951.

The Boston Symphony Orchestra performs the first of what become known as the **Tanglewood Music Festival** concerts in the Berkshires. The orchestra moves to its current home on the former Tappan estate in Lenox in 1937. The auditorium later known as "The Shed" opens there in 1938, and Ozawa Hall, designed by William Rawn, opens in 1994.

1937

Community Boating is founded by Joseph Lee Jr. as a summer program for children from the West End. It is the oldest public sailing program in the country. After sailing from Watt's Boathouse, then from the dock of the Union Boat Club, the club moves to its current boathouse on the Charles River in 1941.

John P. Marquand's Pulitzer Prize–winning novel, *The Late George Apley*, is published. Marquand's biographer, Stephen Birmingham, later describes the book as "a detailed Valentine to a city—Boston—such as no other American city can expect."

1938

March 14. The first issue of the *Mid-Town Journal* appears. Published by **Frederick B. Shibley** from his home at **40 Union Park Street** in the South End, the offbeat publication becomes famous for its 100-word leads and tongue-in-cheek coverage of vice crimes. Its last issue appears on June 6, 1966.

September 21. The **Great New England Hurricane** strikes Boston. The most destructive storm in the city's history, its 130-mile-an-hour winds cause $6 million in damage and deposit enough sand to connect Deer Island to Winthrop.

1939

April 21. The **George Wright Golf Course** is dedicated at **420 West Street** in Hyde Park, with Boston Mayor **Maurice J. Tobin** hitting a 200-yard drive from the first tee. The 18-hole course, designed by Donald Ross, is built as a federal Works Progress Administration project and is named for the former baseball player and manager who later opened a sporting goods store and championed the sport of golf in Boston.

The Washington Street theater district on a snowy night, 1935. (Courtesy of the Bostonian Society, Arthur Hansen Collection)

1940

Spring. **Herbert Philbrick** visits the Boston office of the Federal Bureau of Investigation (FBI) at **7 Water Street**. Soon after, he agrees to become an informant for the agency. For the next nine years, Philbrick joins and reports on alleged Communist infiltration of various Boston-area political groups. His experience becomes the basis for a book and a television series, both entitled *I Led Three Lives.*

Malcolm X (then Malcolm Little) moves to Boston from Detroit, living with his half-sister first on Humboldt Avenue, then at **72 Dale Street** in Roxbury. In *The Autobiography of Malcolm X*, he later writes: "Soon I ranged out of Roxbury and began to explore Boston proper. Historic buildings everywhere I turned, and plaques and markers and statues for famous events and men. One statue in Boston Common astonished me: a Negro named Crispus Attucks, who had been the first man to fall in the Boston Massacre. I had never known anything like it."

The **Cities Service** sign is erected in **Kenmore Square**. The logo of the 60'x60' sign is changed to **CITGO** in 1965. The nearly 5,800 neon glass tubes are replaced by almost 220,000 light-emitting diodes (LEDs) in 2005.

The **Savoy** nightclub opens at **441 Columbus Avenue** in the South End (it later moves to 410 Massachusetts Avenue). The club is known for the quality of the jazz performed there. Then-Northeastern undergraduate Nat Hentoff hosts a live radio program there and later writes: "Behind the closed doors of the Savoy, I felt more at home than anywhere else I had ever been, including home."

Ted Williams is shown here batting in the Red Sox 1947 home opener at Fenway Park. (Courtesy of the Boston Herald)

November 10. A *Boston Sunday Globe* headline reads: "Kennedy Says Democracy All Done in Britain, Maybe Here." In the story, reporter Louis Lyons quotes Ambassador to England **Joseph P. Kennedy** as saying: "There's no sense in our getting in (the war)." Reaction to Kennedy's comments force him to resign his post soon after and dashed any hopes he might have had of running for president himself, and forced him to transfer his political ambitions to his sons.

1941

Robert McCloskey's *Make Way for Ducklings* is published. An Ohio native who studied at Boston's Vesper Art School, McCloskey wins the Caldecott Medal for best children's picture book in 1942. Newton sculptor Nancy Shon's bronze sculpture, *Mrs. Mallard and Her Eight Ducklings* (Jack, Kack, Lack, Mack, Nack, Ouack, Pack, and Quack) is installed in the Public Garden in 1987.

1942

February 10. The Bruins beat the Montreal Canadiens 8–1 at Boston Garden, as the team's so-called **"Kraut Line"** (Woody Dumart, Milt Schmidt, and Bobby Bauer—all from Kitchener, Ontario) scores 11 points in their last game before leaving for service with the Royal Canadian Air Force in World War II.

November 28. A fire destroys the **Cocoanut Grove** nightclub at **17 Piedmont Street** in Park Square and claims 492 lives. It is the greatest tragedy in terms of loss of life in Boston history. Initial reports suggest that the fire started when a 16-year-old busboy lit a match to see in the dark after a customer had loosened a light bulb over a booth to make the setting more romantic. A subsequent investigation casts doubt on that theory and reveals that the club was jammed with more than 1,000 patrons at the time of the fire, twice its legal capacity.

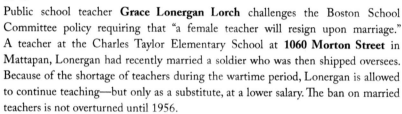

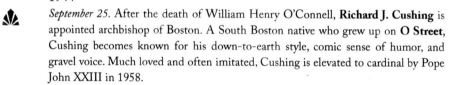

The *Boston Advertiser* headline following the Cocoanut Grove fire, 1942. (Courtesy of the Bostonian Society)

1943

Public school teacher **Grace Lonergan Lorch** challenges the Boston School Committee policy requiring that "a female teacher will resign upon marriage." A teacher at the Charles Taylor Elementary School at **1060 Morton Street** in Mattapan, Lonergan had recently married a soldier who was then shipped oversees. Because of the shortage of teachers during the wartime period, Lonergan is allowed to continue teaching—but only as a substitute, at a lower salary. The ban on married teachers is not overturned until 1956.

1944

September 25. After the death of William Henry O'Connell, **Richard J. Cushing** is appointed archbishop of Boston. A South Boston native who grew up on **O Street**, Cushing becomes known for his down-to-earth style, comic sense of humor, and gravel voice. Much loved and often imitated, Cushing is elevated to cardinal by Pope John XXIII in 1958.

December. Architect **William Roger Greeley**, speaking at **Faneuil Hall**, facetiously bemoans the fact that Boston did not suffer "the advantage of widespread destruction by aerial bombardment," like London. Greeley, who favors the demolition of old buildings and their replacement with new ones, says Boston must "destroy our own diseased tissues and by heroic will-power rebuild our community as a worthy competitor of the newer type of city."

1945

January 4. In a famous—and possibly true—Boston story, firefighters who arrive at the **Somerset Club** at **42 Beacon Street** are directed by Joseph, a club employee, to go around to the service entrance in back. After dinner is over, Joseph announces: "There will be no dessert this evening, gentlemen. The kitchen is on fire."

April 16. After being prodded by sportswriters **Jack Egan** and **Wendell Smith** and Boston City Councilor **Isadore Muchnick**, the Red Sox grant brief tryouts to three African-American players—**Jackie Robinson, Sam Jethro,** and **Marvin Williams.** None of the players is signed to a contract. The Red Sox becomes the last major league team to add an African-American player when infielder **Elijah "Pumpsie" Green** plays his first game for the team on July 21, 1959.

April 29. The **"Battle of the Bricks"** begins on Beacon Hill. A group of residents, described by the *Boston Post* as "Beacon Hill matrons, maintaining their poise and dignity," stages a demonstration on **West Cedar Street** to protest the replacement of their brick sidewalks with concrete. Their protest proves successful and Boston Mayor James Michael Curley later orders the old bricks reinstalled. The demonstration is credited with sparking the preservation movement on Beacon Hill.

Cynthia Belgrave becomes the first African-American clerk at a downtown Boston department store when she is hired to wrap Christmas gifts at Gilchrist's at **417 Washington Street**. Her hiring comes only after African-American residents demonstrate to protest that the only minorities working in downtown Boston stores and offices are elevator operators.

Berklee College of Music is founded by Larry Berk at **284 Newbury Street**. Originally the Schillinger House of Music, the school adopts its current name—an anagram of the founder's son's name—in 1954 and shifts its emphasis to jazz. Larry Berk is the school's first president and is succeeded by his son, Lee, in 1979. The school's graduates would include Gary Burton, Keith Jarrett, Quincy Jones, Patty Larkin, and Branford Marsalis. The school moves to its current location at **150 Massachusetts Avenue** in 1972.

1946

October 15. The **Red Sox** lose to the Cardinals 4–3 in game 7 of the World Series in St. Louis, as Enos Slaughter scores from first base on a double by Harry Walker in the eighth inning. **Johnny Pesky** is later criticized for holding the ball too long before making the relay throw to the plate, but many fault substitute center fielder Leon Culberson for not getting the ball into the infield quickly enough. **Ted Williams** hits only five singles and drives in one run in 25 at-bats in the only World Series in which he would play.

November 5. **John F. Kennedy** wins election to Congress from the 11th Massachusetts District, which includes part of Boston. During his campaign, Kennedy established a residence in Room 308 of the Bellevue Hotel at **21 Beacon Street** on Beacon Hill and admitted that his long absence had made him "a stranger in the city of his birth."

December 9. Jean Cocteau's *The Eagle Rampant*, starring Tallulah Bankhead, opens at the Plymouth Theatre at **131 Stuart Street**. A young **Marlon Brando** is a member of the cast—but only briefly. He is fired after the first performance for overacting in a death scene.

1947

The **"Old" John Hancock Building** opens at **175 Berkeley Street** in the Back Bay. Designed by Cram & Ferguson, the 26-story building is the first "skyscraper" built in

Police investigate the scene of the Brink's robbery. (Courtesy of the Boston Herald/Boston Public Library)

Boston since the Custom House Tower in 1915. The antenna atop the building is first lit in 1950. The colors it flashes indicate the weather according to the following code: "Steady blue, clear view/flashing blue, clouds are due;/steady red, rain ahead/ flashing red, snow instead."

Cleveland Amory's *The Proper Bostonians* is published. The book contains the following passage: "The Proper Bostonian did not just happen; he was planned. Since he was from the start, in that charming Boston phrase "well-connected," he was planned to fit into a social world so small that he could not help being well-defined. He is a charter member of a society which more than one historian has called the most exclusive of that of any city in America, and which has charter members only."

June 26. Boston Mayor **James Michael Curley** is sentenced to serve six to 18 months in federal prison in Danbury, Connecticut, for mail fraud. Because City Council President John Kelly is under indictment for bribery (he is later acquitted), City Clerk John B. Hynes is named acting mayor of Boston. After Curley's sentence is commuted by President Truman (with the entire Massachusetts congressional delegation—except for John F. Kennedy—requesting his release), Curley returns to Boston on Thanksgiving Day and is greeted by a crowd of 5,000 well-wishers at **South Station**. Back at City Hall a day later, he boasts: "I have accomplished more in one day than has been done in the five months of my absence." The remark reportedly infuriates Hynes, and prompts him to run against Curley in the next mayoral election in 1949.*

1948

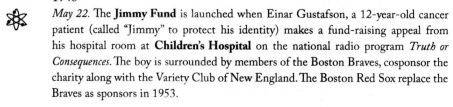

May 22. The **Jimmy Fund** is launched when Einar Gustafson, a 12-year-old cancer patient (called "Jimmy" to protect his identity) makes a fund-raising appeal from his hospital room at **Children's Hospital** on the national radio program *Truth or Consequences.* The boy is surrounded by members of the Boston Braves, cosponsor the charity along with the Variety Club of New England. The Boston Red Sox replace the Braves as sponsors in 1953.

June 9. At 6:15 p.m., **WBZ-TV** broadcasts the first commercial television programming in Boston. Arch MacDonald reads follows 15 minutes of news; congratulations from Catholic, Protestant, and Jewish clergy follow; then the *Kraft Television Theatre* is broadcast to an audience of more than 100,000 viewers.

1949

October 24. "MTA." (popularly known as "Charlie on the MTA") is first performed publicly by the Boston Peoples Artists outside factory gates in Roxbury and South Boston. Written by **Jacqueline Steiner** and **Bess Lomax Hawes,** it is a campaign song for Walter A. O'Brien Jr., the Progressive Party candidate for mayor and an opponent of the recent subway fare increase. The song becomes a big hit for the Kingston Trio in June 1959, but only after they removed O'Brien's name from the lyrics because he had been caught up in the "Red Scare" hysteria of the early 1950s.

November 8. **John B. Hynes** defeats James Michael Curley to win election as mayor of Boston. His election, according to the *Boston Globe,* "marks the end of one era and the beginning of another." It also marks the last time an incumbent Boston mayor is defeated in a bid for re-election.

December 16. **Freedom House** opens. Founded the year before by **Otto** and **Muriel Snowden** and 15 others, it is a social service organization whose goal is to reduce barriers for African-American residents in education, employment, and housing. It later moves to **14 Crawford Street** in Roxbury. Freedom House becomes such an important institution in the civil rights effort in Boston that it comes to be called "The Black Pentagon."

1950

Boston's population is 801,444. It is the 10th largest city in the U.S.

January 17. The **Brink's Robbery** is carried out when thieves wearing Halloween masks rob the company's countinghouse at **600 Commercial Street** in the North End of $2.7 million in cash, checks, securities, and money orders. It is the largest robbery in the U.S. up to this time. The robbers almost commit the perfect crime. But on January 6, 1956—11 days before the state's statute of limitations was to have run out—one of them, Joseph "Specs" O'Keefe, confesses to the robbery and names his cohorts. Only $60,000 of the stolen money is ever recovered, however.

April 25. The Boston Celtics draft **Chuck Cooper** of Duquesne, making him the first

African-American player to be drafted in National Basketball Association (NBA) history. A few weeks before, team owner Walter Brown hired 32-year-old **Red Auerbach** as the team's new coach. The Celtics were founded in 1946 as a member of the Basketball Association of America, which became part of the NBA in 1949.

1951

March 8. Creation of the **Freedom Trail** is suggested by **William Schofield**, who proposes a "Puritan Path" or 'Liberty Loop' or 'Freedom's Way' or whatever you want to call it," in his column in the *Boston Evening Traveler*. Boston Mayor John B. Hynes and business leaders immediately embrace the idea. The Freedom Trail Foundation is established in 1951 and the 16 sites on the 5.5-mile trail are: **Boston Common**, the **Massachusetts State House**, **Park Street Church**, the **Old Granary Burying Ground**, **King's Chapel and Burying Ground**, the site of the original **Boston Latin School** and the **Ben Franklin Statue** on the grounds of **Old City Hall**, the **Old Corner Bookstore**, **Old South Meeting House**, the **Old State House**, the site of the **Boston Massacre**, **Faneuil Hall**, the **Paul Revere House**, the **Old North Church**, **Copp's Hill Burying Ground**, the USS *Constitution*, and the **Bunker Hill Monument**. A red line marking the trail is painted on the sidewalk in 1958.

October 1. The **Chinese Merchants Association Building** (On Leong Building) opens at **2 Tyler Street**. Designed by Edward Chin Park, the building's roof is topped by a Chinese pagoda. Its opening is marked by a weeklong celebration of parades and fireworks. Despite protests from the community, part of the building is demolished to make way for construction of the Central and Surface Arteries in 1953.

1952

November 4. **John F. Kennedy** narrowly defeats **Henry Cabot Lodge Jr.** to win election to the U.S. Senate. After Kennedy's victory, his mother, Rose Fitzgerald Kennedy, reminisces about when her father, John F. Fitzgerald, was a young boy delivering newspapers and had once been given shelter on a winter evening by a cook in the Lodge house at **31 Beacon Street**. "In his wildest dreams that winter's night," she asks, "could he ever have imagined how far both he and his family would come?"

December 26. The first **Beanpot Hockey Tournament** is held at **Boston Arena**, as Boston University beats Northeastern 4–1 and Harvard beats Boston College 3–2 in overtime. The tournament moves to Boston Garden in January 1954, switches to February in 1955, and to the first and second Monday nights in February in 1958. It continues to be held today.

1953

November 9. The **Old Howard Theatre** at **34 Howard Street** in Scollay Square is closed by Boston Municipal Court Judge Elijah Adlow. With evidence obtained by a Boston Police photographer showing the performances of strippers Rose LaRose and Marion Russell, Adlow finds both the two dancers and building's managers guilty of lewdness. The building is badly damaged by a fire in 1961 and torn down to make way for the Government Center urban renewal project in 1962.

Construction of the John F. Fitzgerald Expressway/Central Artery, ca. 1955. (Courtesy of the Bostonian Society, Central Artery Collection)

1954

Sunday, June 6. The Red Sox beat Cleveland 7–4 at **Fenway Park**, as second-year first baseman **Harry Agganis** hits a two-run homer to win the game. Immediately after the game, Agganis rushes to Boston University's commencement exercises, which are being held at the site of the former **Braves Field**, to receive his bachelor's degree. A Lynn native and one of the finest schoolboy athletes in Massachusetts history, Agganis dies a year later from a cerebral pulmonary embolism.

October 26. In a speech entitled "Boston, Whither Goest Thou," Boston Mayor John B. Hynes lays out his vision for a **"New Boston"** at the first Boston College Citizens Seminar in Fulton Hall on the Boston College campus in Chestnut Hill. Mayor Hynes later says that the seminars "pried open windows long and tightly closed." His successor, John F. Collins, says they "helped mightily in knitting together a city which sometimes seemed to find division the natural order."

December 23. **Dr. Joseph Murray** performs the first successful organ transplant in history at **Peter Bent Brigham Hospital**—transferring a kidney donated to Richard Herrick by his identical twin brother, Ronald. Murray is awarded the Nobel Prize in 1990. Richard Herrick later marries a nurse he met in the recovery room after his operation. He dies in 1963.

1955

April 1. **Tony DeMarco** of the North End beats Johnny Saxton with a 14th-round TKO at the **Boston Garden** to win the world welterweight title. The whole neighborhood celebrates the victory of the fighter who grew up only a few blocks from the

arena. DeMarco later loses the title to Carmen Basilio in two fights later in the year that are called among the greatest fights in boxing history.

1956

The **Central Artery** opens through downtown Boston. Wags later joke that its name comes from the fact that it is always "clogged." The highway is later renamed the John F. Fitzgerald Expressway.

Edwin O'Connor's *The Last Hurrah* is published, with a fictional hero, Frank Skeffington, based on James Michael Curley. The book contains the passage: "I think you ought to know something about the city. . . It changed overnight, you know. A hundred years ago the loyal sons and daughters of the first white inhabitants went to bed one lovely evening, and by the time they woke up and rubbed their eyes, their charming old city was swollen to three times its size. The savages had arrived. Not the Indians; far worse. It was the Irish. They had arrived and they wanted in. Even worse than that, they got in. The story of how they did may not be a particularly pretty one on either side, but I doubt if anyone would deny that it was exciting and, as I say, unique. Moreover, it's not quite over yet, though we're in its last stages now."

1957

April 13. The Celtics beat the St. Louis Hawks 125–123 in double overtime in game 7 at **Boston Garden** to win their first NBA championship. The Celtics are led by rookie **Bill Russell**. With Russell as a player, then as player-coach, the Celtics would go on to win 11 championships in the next 13 years, a dynasty unmatched in the history of professional sports.

September. The **Boston Redevelopment Authority** (BRA) is created. One of the only city agencies in the country that supervises both planning and development activities, the BRA assumes control of the city's urban renewal projects from the Boston Housing Authority.

1958

April. The **West End Urban Renewal Project** begins when the Boston Redevelopment Authority seizes 46 acres by eminent domain. Demolition begins in May and is completed in March 1960. More than 4,000 families are displaced and an estimated 2,800 homes torn down. A group headed by Jerome Rappaport, the former personal secretary to Boston Mayor Hynes, is chosen to develop the area and subsequently builds **Charles River Park**, a complex of high-rise luxury apartment buildings. According to historian Walter Muir Whitehill, "The experience of the West End created a widespread conviction that if urban renewal were necessary in Boston, some less drastic form must be devised."

October. **Oliver Smoot Jr.** (MIT '62) is used by his Lamda Chi Alpha fraternity mates to measure the length of the Harvard Bridge ("364.4 Smoots plus one ear") on **Massachusetts Avenue** in the Back Bay. When the bridge is rebuilt in 1990, the "Smoot marks" are repainted every year by Lamda Chi Alpha fraternity pledges.

Demolition of the West End. (Courtesy of the Bostonian Society, Robert B. Severy Collection)

1959

Chiang Yee's *Silent Traveler in Boston* is published. In it, he writes of being told "to be sure to go to see the American room (at the Museum of Fine Arts), for there I would see something which I never could see in any other museum in the world. I would find a group of people under a certain portrait and their family name would be that of the person in the portrait. All Bostonians were like that. They went to the museum to see their ancestors' portrait and never wanted to see any other picture."

The **Boston Coordinating Committee** is formed at a meeting of more than 100 business leaders at the Wayside Inn in Sudbury. Known as "The Vault" because its first meetings were held in the boardroom near the vault of the Boston Safe Deposit Company on **Franklin Street**, the organization is credited with working closely with first Mayor Hynes and then Mayor Collins on issues regarding city finances and development. It is less active in recent years, especially as more Boston companies are bought up by out-of-town corporations, and disbands in 1997.

November 25. Elizabeth Hardwick's essay "**Boston: A Lost Ideal**" appears in *Harper's*. In it, she describes "Boston—wrinkled, spindly-legged, depleted of nearly all her spiritual and cutaneous oils, provincial, self-esteeming—has gone on spending and spending her inflated bills of pure reputation, decade after decade. Now, one supposes it is over at last."

1960

September 9. The **Boston Patriots** lose to the Denver Broncos 13–10 before 21,597 fans at Boston University's Nickerson Field, in the first game in the newly formed American Football League. The team later plays at Fenway Park and Boston College's Alumni Stadium before moving to Foxboro and being renamed the New England Patriots in 1971.

September 22. Boston Mayor **John F. Collins** and newly arrived Boston Redevelopment Authority administrator **Edward J. Logue** announce "A Ninety Million Dollar Development Program for Boston." The plan includes proposals for the redevelopment of downtown Boston as well as many of its neighborhoods.

September 28. Red Sox beat Baltimore 5–4 before 10,454 fans at **Fenway Park**, as **Ted Williams** hits an eighth-inning home run in the last at-bat of his career. In an essay entitled "Hub Fans Bid Kid Adieu," John Updike later describes the scene that followed: "The papers said that the other players, and even the umpires on the field, begged him to come out and acknowledge us in some way, but he never had and did not now. Gods do not answer letters."

November 7. **John F. Kennedy** delivers an electrifying campaign speech to a crowd estimated at 20,000 people at an election-eve rally in **Boston Garden**. Author and Boston native Theodore H. White later describes Kennedy being "surrounded on the dais by a covey of the puffy, pink-faced, predatory-lipped politicians who had so dominated Massachusetts politics before he had taken over." An estimated 100,000 people lined the streets prior to the event. The next day, Kennedy becomes the first Catholic to be elected president of the United States. Inaugurated on January 20, 1961, Kennedy takes the oath of office on a Bible which had belonged to his grandfather, former Boston Mayor John F. Fitzgerald.

1961

The **Pine Street Inn** is established. A refuge for the indigent, alcoholic, and homeless, it is located initially at 8 Pine Street and moves to its current location in the former Boston Fire Department headquarters building at **444 Harrison Avenue** in the South End 1978.

The **Sportsmen's Tennis Club** opens at **930 Blue Hill Avenue** in Dorchester. It is founded by Jimmy and Gloria Smith to introduce inner-city young people to tennis and continues in operation today.

November 18. The **Boston Common Underground Garage** opens. First proposed in 1946, the project is plagued by construction delays, cost overruns, and charges of corruption. The garage is declared structurally unsafe and closed for repairs in 1993 and reopens two years later.

November 30. ***Biography of a Bookie Joint*** airs on network television. Blacked out in Boston due to a pending criminal investigation, the CBS exposé reveals Boston police frequenting the betting operation run from the Swartz Key Shop at **364 Massachusetts Avenue.**

1962

Sam Bass Warner Jr.'s ***Streetcar Suburbs: The Process of Growth in Boston, 1870–1900*** is published. In it, he declares: "Above all else the streetcar suburbs stand as a monument to a society which wished to keep the rewards of capitalist competition open to all its citizens. Despite ignorance and prejudice, during this period of mass immigration, the suburbs remained open to all who could meet the price."

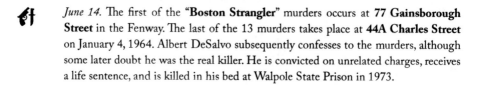

June 14. The first of the **"Boston Strangler"** murders occurs at **77 Gainsborough Street** in the Fenway. The last of the 13 murders takes place at **44A Charles Street** on January 4, 1964. Albert DeSalvo subsequently confesses to the murders, although some later doubt he was the real killer. He is convicted on unrelated charges, receives a life sentence, and is killed in his bed at Walpole State Prison in 1973.

August 27. Democratic U.S. Senate candidates **Edward M. Kennedy** and **Edward J. McCormack Jr.** engage in a debate at South Boston High School at **95 G Street** in South Boston. At one point, McCormack says of his opponent: "If his name was Edward Moore, with his qualifications—with your qualifications, Teddy, your candidacy would be a joke." Kennedy goes on to win the Democratic primary and final election and become one of the most effective and longest-serving U.S. senators in U.S. history.

1963

June 11. **Ruth Batson** and other members of the Boston branch of the NAACP testify that the Boston public schools are engaging in *de facto* segregation at a School Committee meeting at **15 Beacon Street** on Beacon Hill. "We are here," Batson declares, "because the clamor from the community is too anxious to be ignored, the dissatisfaction and complaints too genuine and deep-seated to pass over lightly." A week later, 8,000 African-American students take part in a school boycott to protest segregation, instead attending "Freedom Schools" set up in local churches and community centers.

1964

The term **"Combat Zone"** is first used—by a military police officer—to describe the area along lower **Washington Street** where most of Boston's strip clubs and adult movie houses are located. Boston's zoning code is amended to make that area an official "Adult Entertainment District" in 1974 in an effort to keep such establishments from spreading to other parts of the city.

September 12. **The Beatles** perform for the first time in Boston in a 31-minute concert at **Boston Garden**. The group makes its second and last appearance in Boston at Suffolk Downs in East Boston on August 18, 1966.

1965

April 19. The **Prudential Center** is dedicated at **800 Boylston Street** in the Back Bay in a ceremony attended by an estimated 35,000 people. Designed by Charles Luckman, the 52-story building is the tallest building in the world outside of Manhattan at the time. "Boston was suffering from a major league inferiority complex," former BRA director Stephen Coyle later declares, "and the Pru began the turnaround."

April 23. **Martin Luther King Jr.** leads the **March on Boston**, in which 5,000 people march from Roxbury and a crowd of 20,000 gathers on **Boston Common**. In his speech, King declares: "I would be dishonest to say Boston is Birmingham or that

President John F. Kennedy greets well-wishers on Beacon Hill, 1962. (Courtesy of the Bostonian Society, Walter P. McNaney Collection, Boston Herald photograph)

Massachusetts is a Mississippi. But it would be irresponsible for me to deny the crippling poverty and the injustices that exist in some sections of this community..."

June. **Jonathan Kozol** is fired from the **Christopher Gibson School** at **16 Ronald Street** in Dorchester for teaching the Langston Hughes poem "Ballad of the Landlord." Kozol later writes about his experiences as a teacher in ***Death at an Early Age: The Destruction of the Hearts and Minds of Negro Children in the Boston Public Schools***, which is published in 1967.

August 25. The **MBTA** introduces the "T" logo and color-coded subway lines: Green for the Emerald Necklace; Blue for the ocean; Red for Harvard University; and Orange because Washington Street was formerly called Orange Street.

October 16. The first annual **Head of the Charles Regatta** is held on the Charles River. It subsequently becomes the largest rowing meet in the world.

The prototype of Boston's **Black Heritage Trail** is conceived by Sue Bailey Thurman. The sites eventually include: the **African Meeting House**, the **Smith Court Residences**, the **Abiel Smith School**, the **George Middleton House**, the **Robert Gould Shaw** and **54th Massachusetts Regiment Memorial**, the **Phillips School**, the **John J. Smith House**, the **Charles Street Meeting House**, the **Lewis and Harriet Hayden House**, and the **John Coburn House**.

1966

April 19. **Roberta Gibb** becomes the first woman to complete the **Boston Marathon,** running unofficially since women are still prohibited from taking part. A year later, **Katherine Switzer** runs "officially"—by obtaining a number after applying as "K. Switzer." She nearly has that number torn off her back early in the race by Boston Athletic Association official Jock Semple. But Switzer finishes the race with a time of 4 hours and 20 minutes.

The Standells' single *"Dirty Water"* is released. Written by a Texan and recorded by the Los Angeles band, the song reaches #11 on the national pop music charts on June 11, 1966, and becomes Boston's unofficial rock 'n' roll anthem.

August 10. The **Fort Hill Commune** is established in Roxbury. Formed by friends and followers of musician Mel Lyman, it includes members of the Jim Kweskin Jug Band. The group subsequently purchases a number of houses around Fort Hill Park and, despite Lyman's death in 1978, continues today.

1967

January 17. The **Boston Tea Party** opens at **53 Berkeley Street** in the South End. Boston's first "psychedelic nightclub," it would host performers including The Who, the Velvet Underground, the Grateful Dead, Santana, Led Zeppelin, the Jeff Beck Group, and Traffic. "The opening night of the Tea Party is without a doubt the most important date in Boston rock and roll history," Timothy Crouse later writes. The club moves to 15 Lansdowne Street in 1968 and closes in 1970.

April 6. **William Baird** is arrested for violating Massachusetts law by distributing a contraceptive device to an unmarried 19-year-old female student after speaking at Boston University's Hayden Hall. Baird spends 36 days in Charles Street Jail, but the U.S. Supreme Court later overrules his conviction and strikes down Massachusetts' so-called "Crimes Against Chastity" law in 1972.

June 2–5. The **Grove Hall Riots** break out along a 15-block stretch of Blue Hill Avenue in Roxbury and Dorchester. The violence in the heart of Boston's African-American community is sparked by the arrest of members of a group called Mothers for Adequate Welfare, who had been involved a two-day sit-in at the Grove Hall Welfare Office at **515 Blue Hill Avenue** in Roxbury. Sixty-eight people are reported injured and more than 50 arrested.

October 1. The Red Sox beat the Minnesota Twins 5–3 at **Fenway Park** to win the American League pennant. Dubbed the **"Impossible Dream"** team, because they had finished a half-game out of last place the year before, the Red Sox are led by Triple Crown winner **Carl Yastrzemski.** The Red Sox go on to lose to the St. Louis Cardinals in seven games in the World Series on October 12.

November 7. **Kevin White** defeats **Louise Day Hicks** to win election as mayor of Boston. White had been Massachusetts secretary of state and admitted to seeking the mayor's office in order "to raise money for a gubernatorial bid." Hicks was a

former Boston School Committee member who campaigned on the slogan: "You know where I stand."—a reference to her strong opposition to busing to remedy segregation in the Boston public schools. In the same election, **Thomas I. Atkins** becomes the first African-American to be elected to a citywide spot on the Boston City Council.

1968

May 13. The Boston Banks Urban Renewal Group (**B-BURG**) is launched. Backed by a consortium of 22 banking institutions, the program makes available a $50 million pool of mortgage money to minority families in Boston—but only if they purchase homes in a predominantly Jewish area that includes parts of Roxbury, Dorchester, and Mattapan. Within two years, 40,000 residents of those

Albert DeSalvo in police custody. (Photograph by Dick Thomson, courtesy of the Boston Herald)

neighborhoods move out, and within six years half of all the homes purchased are lost to foreclosure. Hillel Levine and Larry Harmon later write: "The Boston Banks Urban Renewal Group program was to housing what court-ordered desegregation was to education: while creating the impression of fairness, in reality it created more problems than it solved."

June 14. Four members of the so-called "**Boston Five**"—pediatrician Dr. Benjamin Spock, Rev. William Sloane Coffin, Michael Ferber, and Mitchell Goodman, but not Marcus Raskin—are convicted in Federal District Court in Boston of counseling young men to refuse military service. The four are sentenced to two years in prison, but the convictions are overturned by the Federal Court of Appeals in 1969.

September 28. The "**Mothers of Maverick Street**" protest occurs when 25 East Boston women, led by Anna DeFronzo, stage a sit-in on Maverick Street to keep dump trucks bound for Logan Airport from using local streets. After a week of demonstrations, the Massachusetts Port Authority agrees to reroute the truck traffic and subsequently builds a special truck route on airport property.

November 23. "**Harvard beats Yale 29–29**" (according to the next day's *Harvard Crimson*) at Harvard Stadium, when Harvard scores 16 points in the last minute, tying the game on a two-point conversion from substitute quarterback Frank Champi to Pete Varney on the final play.

1969

January 25. An estimated 2,000 people attend a "**People Before Highways**" demonstration on **Boston Common** to protest the proposed construction of the Inner Belt and Southwest Expressway, two megahighways that would have run through

Prudential Center during construction. (Photograph by George Dixon, courtesy of the *Boston Herald*)

downtown Boston. Massachusetts Gov. Francis W. Sargent subsequently reverses the decision to build the highways in 1970.

 October 15. More than 100,000 people protest U.S. involvement in the Vietnam War on **Boston Common**. It is one of the largest of the demonstrations held on this day in cities across the country as part of a **National Vietnam Moratorium**. Among the speakers who address the crowd are U.S. Senators George McGovern of South Dakota and Edward Kennedy of Massachusetts.

1970

May 10. The Boston Bruins beat the St. Louis Blues 4–3 in overtime of game 7 at the **Boston Garden** to win the team's first Stanley Cup in 29 years, as **Bobby Orr** scores the winning goal. The team is also led by **Phil Esposito** ("Jesus Saves . . . and Esposito Scores on the Rebound" is a popular bumper sticker at the time). The Bruins beat the New York Rangers in 1972 to win the team's last Stanley Cup to date.

September 23. Boston Police officer **Walter Schroeder**, a husband and father of nine children, is shot and killed responding to a robbery at the Allston branch of the State Street Bank & Trust Company on **Western Avenue** by a group of self-styled "revolutionaries." The three male robbers are soon arrested, convicted, and sentenced to prison. The two women become fugitives. Susan Saxe surrenders in 1975 and is released from prison in May 1982. Katherine Power surrenders in 1993 and is released from prison in 1999. Schroeder's brother John, also a Boston Police officer, is shot and killed responding to a robbery at a pawn shop at **1904 Washington Street** in Roxbury in 1973.

1971

Corita Kent Mural is painted on one of the two Boston Gas Company tanks on **Commercial Point** in Dorchester. Said to be the largest copyrighted work of art in the U.S., it contains among its rainbow stripes an image that many people believe to be that of North Vietnamese leader Ho Chi Minh—although the artist denied it was

Anti–Vietnam War demonstration, Boston Common. (Photograph courtesy of the Boston Public Library, Print Department)

intentionally a part of the painting. When the larger tank on which it was painted is demolished in 1992, the mural is transferred to the smaller tank in 1994.

George Higgins's mystery novel *The Friends of Eddie Coyle* is published. Among the book's many memorable lines of dialogue is this one: "This life's hard, but it's harder if you're stupid." A movie based on the book is released in 1973.

1972

June. The first annual **Boston Shootout** basketball tournament is held for high school basketball players from around the country. It is organized initially as a showcase for the so-called "Boston Six" (Bobby Carrington, Billy Collins, King Gaskins, Ron Lee, Wilfred Morrison, and Carlton Smith), who make up one of the most talented group of players in the city's history.

December 20. The Boston Housing Authority board votes to turn over management of the Bromley-Heath public housing development to the **Bromley-Heath Tenant Management Corporation** at a meeting at **10 Lamartine Street** in Jamaica Plan. It is reportedly the first time in U.S. history that a tenants group assumes management responsibility for a public housing development. The tenants' group continues to manage the property today.

1973

July 31. A **Delta DC-9** jet crashes while landing in the heavy fog at **Logan Airport**, killing all 89 persons on board. It is the worst aviation disaster in Boston history.

Robert Parker's first "**Spenser**" mystery novel, *The Godwulf Manuscript*, is published. It is the first of what becomes a series of more than 35 books that features a hard-boiled but extremely literate Boston private detective named Spenser, who spells his name "like the English poet."

1974

June 21. **Judge W. Arthur Garrity** rules for the plaintiffs in the *Morgan v. Hennigan* case. In his decision, the judge declares that the Boston School Committee "knowingly carried out a systematic program of segregation" and "intentionally brought about and maintained a dual school system" by creating "Byzantine" feeder systems, "manipulating of district lines and establishing different grade structures for schools in different neighborhoods." A few days later, Judge Garrity

Students being bused to South Boston. (Photograph by Kevin Cole, courtesy of the Boston Herald)

orders "Phase I" of his remedy, which calls for busing thousands of children to schools all over the city in an effort to desegregate the Boston public schools. Opposition to what its detractors call "forced busing" would roil the city for years to come.

July 4. For the first time, the annual **Boston Pops July 4 Concert** on the Esplanade features Tchaikovsky's "1812 Overture", church bells, cannons, and—thanks to businessman David Mugar—fireworks. The event begins to attract hundreds of thousands of spectators and a large television audience, a tradition that continues today.

1975

April 21. **Bill Rodgers** wins his first **Boston Marathon** in a course record time of 2:09. The 27-year-old Boston College graduate wins again in 1978, 1979, and 1980. Rodgers and **Joan Benoit**, a 21-year-old Bowdoin College senior, who wins in a women's record time of 2:35:15 in 1979 and wins the race again in 1983, do much to popularize the Boston Marathon and the sport of running in and around Boston.

June 20. ***Where's Boston?***, a multimedia exhibit, opens in a specially-constructed pavilion at the **Prudential Center** created for the Bicentennial celebration of 1976, the audio/visual treatment of the city's history and neighborhood moves to **60 State Street** in 1978 and continues to be shown until 1988.

1976

April 5. After an antibusing rally on **City Hall Plaza**, a South Boston high school

student uses a flagpole on which an American flag is attached as a weapon in attacking **Theodore Landsmark**, an African-American attorney on his way to a meeting in City Hall. *Boston Herald American* photographer **Stanley Forman** is awarded a Pulitzer Prize for his photograph of the incident, which captures the violence and irony of the controversy over school desegregation in a city known as the Cradle of Liberty.

July 10. As part of the city's Bicentennial celebration, an estimated 650,000 people witness the parade of the **"The Tall Ships"** into **Boston Harbor.** The next day, **Queen Elizabeth II** visits Boston. After touring some of the sites on the Freedom Trail, she speaks from the balcony at the **Old State House**—and is presented a check for $30,000 as reimbursement for the cost of the tea spilled in Boston Harbor in 1773.

August 26. The renovated **Quincy Market** reopens on the 150th anniversary of its original dedication. Designed by Ben Thompson and developed by the Rouse Company, it is also known as **Faneuil Hall Marketplace**. A crowd estimated at 100,000 people spontaneously turns out to tour the building, a reaction the *New York Times* later calls "instant acceptance." The South Market building opens in 1977, the North Market building in 1978.

September 29. The **John Hancock Tower** officially opens at **200 Clarendon Street.** Designed by I.M. Pei and Henry Cobb, the 60-story, 790-foot building is the tallest in Boston. During construction, one-third of its more than 10,000 reflective glass panels shatter and are temporarily replaced with sheets of plywood, but the glass is eventually redesigned and new panels installed. Although initially criticized for dwarfing the smaller, historic buildings in Copley Square, the tower is eventually hailed for its design. As humorist poet Felicia Lamport later writes: "'It's a constant delight to the viewer,'/As someone was recently saying,/'And if the old vistas are fewer,/Well, that is the price I.M. Pei-ing.'"

1977

Alan Lupo's *Liberty's Chosen Home: The Politics of Violence in Boston* is published. It contains the passage: "Boston was not a cosmopolitan city. Its late Yankee literary giants were exceptions to a narrow-minded, parochial, self-serving merchant society. And now, the ethnics were in charge of the same parochial town—each claiming pride in a neighborhood or in a section of a neighborhood. In power, they were, but with less power than their predecessors and therefore, even more protective of what little they had. The tightly knit, parochial neighborhoods were at once the boast and the bane of Boston. They gave the city a quality that most other cities had lost, yet to keep that quality, they forced their sons and daughters inward, to keep their own kind."

Russell Adams's *The Boston Money Tree: How the Proper Men of Boston Made, Invested & Preserved Their Wealth From Colonial Days to the Space Age* is published. It contains the passage: "As the first city to make large amounts of money, Boston became also the first city to grow preoccupied with conserving it."

Donna Summer's hit single "Love to Love You, Baby" reaches the #1 spot on the

A Bicentennial event in front of Faneuil Hall, July 1976. From left to right: Massachusetts Governor Michael Dukakis, his wife, Kitty, Boston Mayor Kevin White, Queen Elizabeth II, and Prince Philip. (Photograph by Frank Hill, courtesy of the *Boston Herald*)

popular music charts. A graduate of Burke High School at **60 Washington Street** in Dorchester, the former LaDonna Gaines also achieves #1 hits with "MacArthur Park" in 1978 and "Bad Girls" in 1979.

1978

February 6. The **Blizzard of '78** strikes Boston. Snow falls for 33 hours, dropping a then record 27.1 inches during one 24-hour period—on top of the 21.4 inches that had previously fallen on January 20. The city is paralyzed for days, but residents find consolation by taking advantage of their isolation to socialize more with their neighbors.

September 5. **Downtown Crossing** (originally the Washington Street Mall) opens along **Washington Street**. The pedestrian mall is created to promote retail business. The Downtown Crossing Association is subsequently formed to coordinate activities and serve as a liaison with the city government in 1980.

1979

February 20. This Old House, a home improvement show, first airs on WGBH-TV Channel 2. The first series of shows features the renovation of a Victorian house on

Meetinghouse Hill in Dorchester. TimeWarner acquires the program from WGBH-TV in 2001 and it continues on the air today.

September 11. The **Boston Resident Jobs Policy** is signed. An executive order proposed by **Chuck Turner** and others, it sets hiring goals of 50% residents, 25% minorities, and 10% women on all major publicly supported construction projects in the city. Although struck down by the Massachusetts Supreme Judicial Court, it is subsequently upheld by the U.S. Supreme Court and is expanded to include major private construction projects in the city in 1985.

October 1. **Pope John Paul II** visits Boston. Two million people line the papal motorcade route and 400,000 people gather in the rain on **Boston Common** to attend a Mass celebrated there by the pope.

1980
September 21. Boston celebrates the **350th Anniversary** of its founding. An 1800-pound birthday cake is unveiled and cut into pieces for 15,000 people on Boston Common in the morning. A parade in which 20,000 people march and more than 1 million people watch is held in the afternoon. The Boston Pops plays for an estimated 120,000 people at City Hall Plaza in the evening.

1981
April 20. **Dick Hoyt** and his son, **Rick Hoyt**, an 18-year-old who is confined to a wheelchair due to cerebral palsy, run their first Boston Marathon together. Except for two years, they have run every year since.

May 4. Law enforcement officers raid the offices of **Gennaro Angiulo** at **98 Prince Street** in the North End, where they had earlier planted an electronic surveillance device. The reputed head of organized crime in Boston, Angiulo is subsequently arrested, tried, and convicted of racketeering, gambling, loan-sharking, and obstruction of justice. He is sentenced to 45 years in prison in February 1986.

1982
September 30. The first episode of the network television show *Cheers* airs. A situation comedy, the show is set in a fictional Boston neighborhood bar modeled after the Bull & Finch Pub at **84 Beacon Street** on Beacon Hill. It becomes the #1-rated show on television. The last episode, one of the most-watched shows in television history, airs on May 20, 1993.

November 20. In one of their most successful "hacks" (practical jokes), students from the **Massachusetts Institute of Technology** (MIT) inflate a weather balloon on the 46-yard line of the football field at **Harvard Stadium** during halftime of the Harvard-Yale game.

December 17. The City of Quincy files suit against the Metropolitan District Commission (MDC) to halt the discharge of untreated sewage into **Boston Harbor**.

The Hampshire House, 84 Beacon Street, the downstairs pub of which served as a model for the television series Cheers.
(Photograph by Richard Tourangeau)

The regional office of the federal Environment Protection Agency files a similar suit in 1985. A cleanup of the harbor is ordered, which is carried out by a new agency, the Massachusetts Water Resources Authority, created in 1984.

1983

November 15. **Ray Flynn** defeats **Mel King** to win election as mayor of Boston. Described during the campaign as the two candidates "duking it out for the vote of the dispossessed, the little guy," both are the sons of dockworkers whose families had at one time been forced to go on welfare. King is the first African-American candidate for mayor to qualify for a final election in Boston history. Flynn is the first candidate from South Boston to be elected and would go on to become known as the "Mayor of the Neighborhoods."

December 20. The Boston Zoning Commission adopts the so-called "**Linkage Ordinance**," which requires developers of large commercial projects downtown to contribute to the construction of affordable housing in the city's neighborhoods. The linkage ordinance is expanded to include contributions to job training programs in 1986.

1984

April 15. The first **Sam Adams Beer** is sold in Boston by the Boston Beer Company, founded by Jim Koch and Rhonda Kallman. The beer is initially brewed in Koch's kitchen and sold in loose bottles delivered by Koch in his station wagon to more than 30 bars in Boston on Patriot's Day. The company today operates a research brewery in the former Haffenreffer Brewery at **30 Germania Street** in Jamaica Plain.

November 23. The Boston College football team beats Miami 47–45 in Miami, as

Doug Flutie throws a 46-yard "**Hail Mary**" touchdown pass to Gerard Phelan on the last play of the game. Flutie is named winner of the Heisman trophy as the outstanding collegiate football player in the country this year and Boston College goes on to beat the University of Houston 45–28 in the Cotton Bowl on January 1, 1985.

1985

March. The New Kids on the Block perform in public for the first time—lip-synching to demo tapes at a concert at the Joseph Lee School at **155 Talbot Avenue** in Dorchester. Originally called Nynuk, the band is made up of five teenage boys from Boston—Jordan and Jonathan Knight, Joey McIntyre, Donnie Wahlberg, and Danny Wood. The group releases its first album a year later and goes on to become popular around the world. After disbanding in 1994, the group reunites in 2008 and continues to play occasional concerts.

Anthony Lukas's ***Common Ground: A Turbulent Decade in the Lives of Three American Families*** is published. It contains the passage: "On June 27, 1974—six days after he had adopted the state plan as the first-stage remedy for Boston—Garrity announced from the bench, 'I saw the state plan for the first time late yesterday afternoon.' To some critics, this was a damaging admission that he had adopted the plan without even reading it. But it was scarcely an inadvertent remark, for Garrity repeated it several times that day. In retrospect, his strategy seems clear. . . by stressing his ignorance of its details, Garrity seemed to be saying, 'If, as some predict, this plan provokes violence in the fall, don't blame me.'"

1986

June 8. The **Boston Celtics** beat the Houston Rockets 114–97 in game 6 at **Boston Garden** to win their 16th championship. The team is led by the "Big Three" of Larry Bird, Kevin McHale, and Robert Parrish and fields what many believe is the greatest basketball team in history.
October 25. After leading 5–3 with two outs in the 10th inning, the **Red Sox** lose to the New York Mets 6–5 in game 6 of the World Series in New York when first baseman **Bill Buckner** allows a ground ball to roll through his legs, enabling the winning run to score. Red Sox Manager John McNamara is criticized afterwards for not making a defensive replacement for Buckner—and criticized two days later when the Red Sox lose game 7 for taking starting pitcher Roger Clemens out of the game too early—or for allowing Clemens to take himself out of the game.

November 4. Voters in predominantly African-American neighborhoods reject by a 3–1 margin a referendum proposal to secede from Boston and create a new city—to be called **Mandela**. The question is again defeated by an even wider margin on November 8, 1988.

1987

January 14. In a meeting at Vanessa's sandwich shop in the Prudential Center at **800 Boylston Street**, three Boston gangsters attempt to extort $500,000 from **Harry "Doc" Sagansky**, 89, reputed to be the top bookie in Boston. Sagansky attempts to

Ray Flynn and Mel King, the 1983 mayoral election finalists.
(Photograph by Michael Grecco, courtesy of the *Boston Herald*)

dismiss their threat, explaining that at his age, "I don't even buy green bananas." But he subsequently complies and begins making the demanded payments.

1988

July 6. **City Year** is founded in Boston by recent Harvard Law School graduates Michael Brown and Michael Khazei. The service organization for recent high school graduates later expands to other cities across the United States.

July 20. Massachusetts Governor **Michael S. Dukakis** wins the Democratic nomination for president at the Democratic National Convention in Atlanta. Six weeks later, his Republican opponent, Vice President **George H. W. Bush**, comes to Boston to campaign tours Boston Harbor and declares it to be "the filthiest harbor in America" on September 1 and goes on to defeat Dukakis and be elected president on November 8.

1989

October 23. Police receive a call from a man on a car phone who identifies himself as **Charles Stuart** and says: "I've been shot. My wife's been shot." They soon locate the car on **St. Alphonsus Street** on Mission Hill. Stuart's wife and unborn child die from the gunshot wounds. He barely survives and later claims that he and his wife were the victims of an African-American attacker. A few months later, however, Stuart's brother confesses to retrieving a gun from him right after the shooting and the next day, January 4, 1990, Stuart's body is found in the water below the **Tobin Bridge**—an apparent suicide. Boston Police and city officials are later criticized for believing Stuart's story and for the manner in which they conducted their investigation of the bizarre case.

1990

May 30. The Boston's **Women's Heritage Trail** opens. Initially a single trail honoring the accomplishments of 20 women, it grows to a number of trails in various neighborhoods honoring more than 50 women.

March 3. "**The Wall**" is erected at the Chez Vous roller-skating rink at **11 Rhoades Street** in Dorchester. A plywood "memorial" created by the Rev. Bruce Wall and rink owners John and Dorcas Dunham, it contains the names of 61 Boston teenagers killed since 1984. Boston ends the year with a record 152 homicides, the result of an epidemic of "crack" cocaine, the increased availability of handguns, and competition among youth gangs for control of drug-dealing activities.

March 18. The Isabella Stewart **Gardner Museum** at **280 The Fenway** is robbed by two thieves dressed as police officers on a Sunday evening at 10 p.m. After gaining entry to the museum, the thieves overpower and tie up security guards, then make off with 13 artworks, including paintings by Vermeer, Rembrandt, Manet, and Degas. The stolen art—later valued by some experts at more than $500 million and by others as "priceless"—has never been recovered.

1991

June 15. **Post Office Square Park** is dedicated. Built on the site of a former parking garage, the park is renamed for Boston developer **Norman B. Leventhal**, who was the driving force behind the park's creation. Leventhal later donates $10 million to the Boston Public Library, the largest gift in the library's history, for a permanent endowment to what is renamed the Norman B. Leventhal Map Center.

1992

May 14. A young man is attacked while attending the funeral of a murder victim at the **Morning Star Baptist Church** at **1257 Blue Hill Avenue** in Mattapan. In response, the **Ten Point Coalition** is established a few days later by a group of African-American ministers. The organization takes its name for the 10-point plan it issues that calls for increased public safety, economic development, and community building in the neighborhoods affected by the continuing scourge of youth violence.

The **Charlestown After Murder Program** (CHAMP) is founded by family members of victims of violence. Its goal is to end the so-called "code of silence" in the neighborhood, which keeps residents from testifying against local criminals.

1993

July 12. Boston Mayor Ray Flynn resigns to become U.S. Ambassador to the Vatican and Boston City Council President **Thomas M. Menino** becomes acting mayor. Dubbed "The Urban Mechanic" for his focus on delivering basic services, Menino goes on to win a special election on November 2 and becomes the longest-serving mayor in Boston history.

1994

March 20. The **St. Patrick's Day Parade** in South Boston is canceled when a Massachusetts court rules that a gay, lesbian, and bisexual group cannot be kept from marching. The U.S. Supreme Court later overrules that decision, declaring that because the South Boston Allied War Veterans is a private group it can exclude groups it feels do not promote its values.

June 19. The ***Boston Globe***—which was awarded a Pulitzer Prize for what was described as "its massive and balanced coverage of the Boston school desegregation conflict"—admits in an editorial that the newspaper was wrong to have supported busing. "Twenty years ago this newspaper unequivocally endorsed a desegregation plan for Boston schools that included busing students between black and white neighborhoods," the newspaper declares, ". . . (but) busing has been a failure in Boston. It achieved neither integration nor better schooling."

1995

January 4. Federal warrants are sworn out for the arrest of three of the top alleged organized crime members in Boston—Stephen "The Rifleman" Flemmi, "Cadillac" Frank Salemme, and **James "Whitey" Bulger**. Flemmi is arrested in Boston the next day. Salemme is arrested in Florida eight months later. But Bulger, brother of Massachusetts Senate President William M. Bulger, appears to have been tipped off that the indictments were being handed down and flees Boston. He remains a fugitive until 2011.

March 19. **John Powers**' article "How to speak with a Bawstin accent: It's not so bzah when you know how" appears in the *Boston Sunday Globe*. In it, the author declares: "Henry Higgins could have taught Eliza Doolittle to tawk Bawstin in a mattah of owahs." The article is expanded to a book, *The Boston Dictionary*, illustrated by Peter Wallace, that is published in 1996.

1996

January. The **Greater Boston Interfaith Organization** is established. A coalition of religious congregations, its goal is to promote solutions to social problems like the lack of affordable housing and the increase in youth violence. Lew Finfer is the first director.

February 1. George Walker's ***Lilacs, for voice and orchestra*** is given its world premiere by the Boston Symphony Orchestra, Seiji Ozawa conducting. Walker is later awarded a Pulitzer Prize for the piece, the first African-American classical music composer so honored.

1997

September 3. The **West End Place at Lowell Square** housing development opens at **150 Staniford Street**. Built by the Archdiocese of Boston, it is the first affordable housing built in the area since the neighborhood was torn down as part of an urban renewal project in 1960. Although former West End residents sought preference for all of the 183 units, a U.S. District court judge later rules that, due to federal Fair Housing regulations enacted since that time, residents displaced from the neighborhood could receive priority for just over half of the units.

December 31. Boston ends the year with 43 homicides, 18 less than the previous year and 109 less than the record number killed in 1990. The **"Boston Miracle"** of improved law enforcement and social service delivery and a better relationship between the police and the community are credited for the decline. The homicide rate continues to decline for two more years but then begins to rise again.

1998

June 28. The **Irish Famine Memorial** is unveiled at 301 Washington Street in Downtown Crossing. Created by sculptor Robert Shure, the statues commemorate the 150th anniversary of the Irish Famine, which killed 1 million people in Ireland and caused another million to flee the country—over 100,000 of whom came to Boston between 1845 and 1849.

The Leonard P. Zakim–Bunker Hill Bridge. (Photograph by Richard Tourangeau)

1999

March. Boston magazine devotes an issue to "**The 12 Tribes of Boston**." The magazine identifies them as: Brahmin, Irish, Black, Jewish, Euro, Italian, Medical, Techno, Culinary, Gay, Intellectual, and Lost (those who inexplicably move to New York). "Because tribalism means that one group often refuses to acknowledge the value of another," the magazine declares, "it can reduce the city to less than the sum of its extraordinary parts."

Northeastern University freshman **Shawn Fanning** creates **Napster**, a program that enables the sharing of music files over the Internet. Asked later why he wrote the software program, Fanning declares: "I was bored. I had some free time." The program becomes incredibly popular with young people but is criticized by the music industry and many artists, and various courts order Napster to be shut down in 2001.

2000

The Boston Foundation publishes *The Wisdom of Our Choices: Boston's Indicators of Progress, Change and Stability*. The report provides a scorecard—to be updated yearly—in order to indicate how much progress the city is making in areas like housing, the environment, education, the economy, public health, cultural life, civic health, public safety, technology, and transportation. Founded in 1915 as the Permanent Charity Fund of Boston, the Boston Foundation's goal is to build and sustain "a vital, prosperous city and region, where justice and opportunity are extended to everyone."

2001

Thomas H. O'Connor's book *The Hub* is published. It contains the passage: "The 'Old Boston'—the Boston as we have known it in history and in literature—no longer exists. Some time ago it ceased to be the Boston of John Winthrop, Josiah Quincy, or James Jackson Storrow. . . [I]t is equally clear that it is no longer the Boston of John Francis Fitzgerald, James Michael Curley, or John F. Kennedy. . . All that may be wonderfully romantic and nostalgic, but it is now part of the city's past, not of its future. Instead of Yankees, Irish, and Italians, Boston is increasingly populated by African-Americans, Hispanic Americans, and Asian Americans—these are our 'new Bostonians.'"

September 11. Terrorists hijack **American Airlines Flight 11** and **United Airlines Flight 175** after the two planes leave Logan Airport and crash them into the World Trade Center towers in New York, killing more than 2,700 people.

2002

January 19. The **New England Patriots** beat the Oakland Raiders 16–13 in Foxborough in an AFC playoff game, as **Adam Vinatieri** kicks a 45-yard field goal in a driving snowstorm to tie the game at the end of regulation time and a 23-yarder in overtime to win it. The Patriots go on to beat the St. Louis Rams 20–17 in New Orleans to win Super Bowl XXXVI, as Vinatieri kicks a 48-yard field goal on the last play of the game on February 3. The team also wins the Super Bowl in 2004 and 2005, against the Carolina Panthers and Philadelphia Eagles, respectively.

October 4. The **Leonard P. Zakim–Bunker Hill Bridge** is dedicated. Designed by Christian Menn, it is the world's widest cable-stayed bridge. When the bridge is open to pedestrians only on May 12, a crowd of 200,000 people walks across it. When the pedestrian-only day is repeated on October 6, 800,000 people turn out.

December 13. Cardinal **Bernard Law** resigns as archbishop of Boston in the wake of a sexual abuse scandal Massachusetts attorney general later finds involved over 700 documented cases of molestation by 250 priests in the Boston archdiocese over a period of more than 60 years.

2003

March 29. The **"Big Dig"** opens to northbound traffic. The largest public works project in U.S. history, the depression of the formerly elevated Central Artery opens to southbound traffic on December 20. Although the cost of the project escalated to more than triple its expected price, the knitting together of the city's downtown, opening up of the waterfront, and creation of more than 20 acres of parkland was a welcome addition to the city.

2004

July 28. Senator **John F. Kerry** (D-Mass.) wins his party's nomination for president at the Democratic National Convention, which is held at the Fleet Center, a short walk from his Beacon Hill home. It is the first national political convention ever held in Boston. Kerry loses to incumbent Republican President George W. Bush in the general election on November 2.

New England Patriot Adam Vinatieri kicks the game-winning field goal against the Oakland Raiders at Foxborough Stadium, January 2002. (Photograph by Michael Seamans, courtesy of the *Boston Herald*)

 October 20. The **Red Sox** beat the New York Yankees 10–3 in game 7 of the American League championship series at Yankee Stadium to become the first team in baseball history to win a playoff series after losing the first three games. The Red Sox—a self-styled "Bunch of Idiots" led by Johnny Damon, Kevin Millar, David Ortiz, and Manny Ramirez—go on to beat the Cardinals 3–0 in game 4 in St. Louis on October 27 to win the team's first World Series since 1918. The Red Sox beat the Colorado Rockies to win another World Series in 2007.

2005

January 23. On a Sunday in January, when two feet of snow fall on Boston and the New England Patriots are playing for the American Football Conference championship, 123 Boston Police officers and a record 109 Boston firefighters—nearly one-fourth of the total shift—call in sick and fail to report for work.

May 20. Fifty-five same-sex couples are wed during the course of the day by a team made up of two ministers and one rabbi at the Arlington Street Church at **351 Boylston Street** in the Back Bay. In 2003, the Massachusetts Supreme Judicial Court—by a 4–3 margin—had ruled in *Goodridge v. Department of Public Health* that state laws excluding same-sex couples from marriage were unconstitutional. A year later, in an advisory opinion decided by a similar margin, the court declared that the only way to meet the state constitution's guarantee of equal rights was to grant same-sex couples full marriage rights.

2006

April 13. **Kai Leigh Harriott**, a five-year-old girl who two years earlier had been shot and left paralyzed from the waist down by a stray bullet while playing on the porch of her home on **Bowdoin Street** in Dorchester, makes a victim-impact statement in Boston Superior Court after the man who fired the shot pleads guilty to assault and battery with a deadly weapon. "What you done to me was wrong," she tells the man who fired the shot and has just pled guilty to assault and battery with a deadly weapon. Then, turning to the judge, Harriott says "but I still forgive him." The man is sentenced to 13–15 years in prison. As he is led from court, Kai's mother, **Tonya David**, shakes the man's handcuffed hand and embraces him.

2007

January 31. An investment banker pays $23 million for two buildings at **196 Commonwealth Avenue** and **25 Exeter Street** that he plans to join together to create the largest single-family home in Boston, a 23,000-square-foot double townhouse with 15 bathrooms. Two years later, a parking spot behind **48 Commonwealth Avenue** is purchased by an unidentified buyer for a $300,000, a record price for a parking space in Boston. Five months after that, the owner of the penthouse at the Mandarin Oriental Residences at **778 Boylston Street** puts his condominium on the rental market for $52,000 a month, the highest asking rent ever in Boston.

2008

October 5. The **Rose Kennedy Greenway** is dedicated. The 13.5-acre, mile-long park is named for Mrs. Kennedy, who was born in the North End and was the mother of a president and two U.S. senators. The park is built atop the now-underground highway formerly called the John F. Fitzgerald Expressway, which was named for her father, a former mayor of Boston.

2009

August 29. A funeral Mass is held for Sen. **Edward M. Kennedy** at Mission Church at **1525 Tremont Street** on Mission Hill. Kennedy died at his home in Hyannisport on

Construction on the Big Dig. (Photograph by Mike Adaskaveg, courtesy of the *Boston Herald*)

August 25. His wake at the John F. Kennedy Library on Columbia Point in Dorchester was attended by thousands of admirers and his funeral is attended by President Barack Obama and former U.S. presidents Jimmy Carter, Bill Clinton, and George W. Bush.

June 26. The **Islamic Society of Boston Cultural Center and Mosque** opens at **1 Malcolm X Boulevard** in Roxbury. An estimated 1,800 people attend the afternoon worship service.

2010

Boston's population is 617,594; 53% of the population is classified as nonwhite, the second decade in a row that Boston is classified as a "majority-minority" city. The increase in the total population from the previous decade is 4.8% and marks the first time that Boston's population growth exceeded that of the metropolitan area (3.1%) and the first time in 130 years that it exceeded that of the state (3.1%).

February 4. The **State Street Corporation** at **1 Lincoln Street** agrees to pay more than $300 million in restitution and fines for failing to inform clients about high-risk investments in subprime, mortgage-backed bonds. The company dates from 1792 and is the second oldest financial institution in continuous existence in Massachusetts. The investors who had been harmed by the risky investments include approximately 50 Massachusetts charities, religious groups, schools, and pension systems.

Michael Rawson's *Eden on the Charles* is published. The book contains the passage: "It is always hard to say that there's a particular culture in one city that's had continuity over centuries, but it's more possible to say it of Boston. It's a place where the search for environmental permanence was born, at least for America, versus just tearing things down."

2011

January 6. For the first time in memory, the Massachusetts Division of Marine Fisheries allows a small group of "master diggers" to remove shellfish from Boston Harbor at **Malibu Beach** in Dorchester. The granting of such permission illustrates the progress made in cleaning up what 23 years earlier had been called "the filthiest harbor in America."

June 15. The **Boston Bruins** beat the Vancouver Canucks 4–0 at Rogers Arena in Vancouver to win the team's first Stanley Cup in 39 years. With the victory, Boston becomes the first city to win each of the four major professional sports championships within a span of seven years.

June 22. **James "Whitey" Bulger** is arrested by FBI agents in Santa Monica, California, after spending more than 16 years as a fugitive. While he was on the run, the original racketeering indictment against him was replaced by another charging him with 19 murders. Bulger is returned to Boston and is currently being held in the Plymouth County Correctional Facility while awaiting trial.

September 30. The **Occupy Boston** protest begins on part of the **Rose Kennedy Greenway** in front of the Federal Reserve Building. Part of a nationwide movement, the demonstration eventually consists of several hundred people—many of them college students—camping out in tents to protest unfair financial practices by the government and private sector. The Boston demonstration lasts longer than those in other cities, but due to complaints of damage to the park and concerns over health and safety, the protesters are eventually evicted from the site on December 10, 2011.

2012

February 5. The **New England Patriots** lose to the New York Giants 21–17 at Lucas Oil Stadium in Indianapolis in Superbowl XLVI. In losing, the team fails to avenge their loss to the Giants in Superbowl XLII, which prevented the Patriots from becoming only the second undefeated team in NFL history.

August 19. The USS *Constitution* celebrates the 200th anniversary of its victory over the HMS *Guerriere* by sailing briefly under its own power in Boston Harbor.

INDEX

Frog Pond, 38
Fuller, Margaret, 56, 58, 60
Funk and Wilcox, 105

G

G&G Delicatessen, 108
Gage, Thomas, 34
Gandil, Chick, 105
garbage, 10
Gardner, Isabella Stewart, 86, 96
Gardner, Jack, 86
Gardner Museum, 139
Garrison, William Lloyd, 45, 54, 56, 58, 63, 70
Garrity, W. Arthur, 132
George Wright Golf Course, 114
Georges Island, 19
Gerry, Elbridge, 47
"Gerrymander," 47
Gibb, Roberta, 128
Gilchrist's, 118
Gillette, King, 90
Gilman, Arthur, 74
Gilmore Bridge, 37
Gilmore, Patrick Sarsfield, 76
Globe Theatre, 56, 85
Gloss, George and Ken, 50
Glover, Mary "Goody," 16
Gold Rush, 64
Goldstein, Charlie, 108
golf tee, invented, 94
Good Government Association, 96
Goodridge v. Department of Public Health, 144
Goodwin, James, 22
Gorges, Robert, 1
Gourlay, Robert, 60
Granary Burying Ground, 11, 24, 32, 36, 121
Grant, George Franklin, 94
grasshopper weathervane, 27, 47

Gray, Horace, 57
Gray, Samuel, 32
"Great Awakening," 27
Great Boston Fire, 78
Great Bridge, 11
Great Elm, 80
Great Fire of 1711, 20, 21
Great New England Hurricane, 114
Great Snow, 22
Great Tide, 20
Greater Boston Interfaith Organization, 140
Greeley, William Roger, 117
Green Dragon Tavern, 14
Green, Elijah "Pumpsie," 118
Green, Irving, 108
Greene, Nathaniel, 30
Grenville Acts, 30
Grenville, Henry, 24
Griffin's Wharf, 33
Grimké, Angelina, 57, 76
Grimké, Sarah, 76
Grove Hall, 43
Grove Hall Riots, 128
Guardian, 95
Gustafson, Einar, 120

H

Haffenreffer Brewery, 136
Hale, Edward Everett, 5, 57, 62
Hall, Mina, 91
Hall, Primus, 37
Hall, Prince, 11, 37
Halley's Comet, 15
Hancock, Dorothy, 35
Hancock, Ebenezer, 21
Hancock, John, 5, 11, 25, 26, 31, 35, 39
Hancock Tower, 133
Handel and Haydn Society, 48
Handlin, Oscar, 58
Harcourt Building, 97
Hardwick, Elizabeth, 124
Harmon, Larry 129

Harriott, Kai Leigh, 144
Harris, Benjamin, 15, 16
Harrison, Peter, 28, 29
Hartford Convention, 47
Hart's shipyard, 40
Harvard Medical School, 36, 65, 98, 108
Harvard Stadium, 86, 97
Harvard University, 6, 15, 19, 52, 55, 57, 73, 78, 81, 84, 87, 89, 90, 94, 95, 97, 98, 100, 106, 107, 108, 109, 111, 127, 129, 135, 138
Harvard, John, 6
Harvard-Boston Aero Meet, 101
Hassam, Childe, 93
Hawthorne, Nathaniel, 58
Hayden House, 127
Hayden, Lewis, 64, 66
Hayes, Roland, 104
Head of the Charles Regatta, 127
Hecht House, 87
Hecht, Mrs. Jacob, 87
Hemenway, Harriet, 91
Hendricks Club, 85
Hentoff, Nat, 115
Herrick, Richard and Ronald, 122
Hicks, Louise Day, 128
Higgins, George, 131
Higginson, Henry Lee, 84
Higginson, Thomas Wentworth, 69, 75
high school for girls, 51
Ho Chi Minh, 69, 130
Holmes, Oliver Wendell, 38, 55, 57, 62, 68, 70, 71, 78, 85, 90
Homer, Horatio J., 81
Hong Far Low Restaurant, 82
horsecar line, 69
Horticultural Hall, 53
Hotel Brunswick, 107

R

Railroad Jubilee, 66
Ramirez, Manny, 143
Rand, Sally, 62
Rappaport, Jerome, 123
"Rat Day," 104
Rawson, Michael, 145
Regina Pizza, 109
Regulating Act, 33
Revere Paul, 3, 11, 14, 23, 25, 30, 34, 39, 41, 71, 112
Revolutionary War, 21, 34
Richards, Ellen Swallow, 78
Richardson, H.H., 80
Rickard, George Lewis "Tex," 110
Riley, Thomas, 84
Ripley, George, 56, 58
Ritz-Carlton Hotel, 110
Riverside Press, 83
Roberts v. City of Boston, 63
Roberts, Benjamin, 63
Roberts, Sarah, 63
Robinson, Jackie, 117
Robinson, William, 11
Rock, John Swett, 74
Rodgers, Bill, 132
Rogers, Isaiah, 53, 59, 62
Rogers, Will, 58, 95
Rold's Pistol Gallery, 74
Roosevelt, Franklin Delano, 101, 112
Ropewalk Building, 58
Rose Kennedy Greenway, 144, 146
Roslindale, 79, 86, 87
Ross, Donald, 92
Rouse Company, 133
Rowlandson, Mary, 13
Roxbury, 12, 14, 27, 28, 40, 43, 68, 72, 82, 84, 96, 115, 120, 126, 128, 129, 130, 145
Roxbury Latin School, 8, 12
Royal Exchange Tavern, 24
Royal Province of Massachusetts Bay, 16

Ruffin, Josephine St. Pierre, 89
Ruggles Station, 80
Russell, Bill, 123
Russell, James, 14
Russell, Marion, 121
Ruth, Babe, 106

S

Sabine, Wallace Clement, 95, 97
Sacco, Nicola, 110
"Sacred Cod," 36
Sagansky, Harry "Doc," 139
St. Botolph Club, 86, 97
Saint-Gaudens, Augustus, 92
Saint-Gaudens, Louis, 90
St. James Hotel, 75
St. Patrick's Day, 25, 95, 139
Salemme, "Cadillac" Frank, 140
Sam Adams Beer, 136
Samuel the Jew, 17
Santayana, George, 5
Sargeant, Peter, 14
Sargent, Francis W., 130
Sargent, John Singer, 86, 90, 99
Saturday Club, 68
Savoy Nightclub, 115
Saxe, Susan, 130
Schofield, William, 121
Schouler, William, 6
Schriftgiesser, Kurt, 61
Schroeder, John, 128
Schroeder, Walter, 128
Scollay Square, 15, 60, 62, 99, 121
Sears, David, 66, 81
Sears, William T., 96
Second Church in Boston, 9
"Secret Six," 69
Semple, Jock, 128
September 11, 2001, 142
Sewall, Samuel, 16, 19
Shand-Tucci, Douglass, 37

Shaw, Lemuel, 63
Shaw, Quincy A., 75
Shaw, Robert Gould, 72, 92, 127
Shawmut, 2
Shawmut Peninsula, 3
Shepley, Rutan, and Coolidge, 86, 94
Shibley, Frederick B., 114
Shirley, William, 28, 29
Shirley-Eustis House, 28
shoomakers, first labor organization in America, 9
Shurcliff, Arthur, 112
Shurcliff, Mrs. Arthur, 108
Shure, Robert, 141
Siege of Boston, 24, 29, 30, 33
Simco's on the Bridge, 113
Sims, Thomas, 66
slavery, 6, 15, 19, 25, 31, 32, 36, 53, 54, 56, 57, 64, 66, 68, 69, 70, 103, 106
smallpox, 1, 22, 28, 59
Smibart, John, 25, 27
Smith (Abiel) School, 56, 127
Smith Court Residences, 127
Smith House, 127
Smith, John, 1
Smith, Jerome V. C., 68
Smith, Jimmy and Gloria, 125
Smith, Samuel, 30
Smith, Wendell, 117
smoking, first prohibited, 4
Smoot, Oliver Jr., 123
Snodgrass, Emma, 67
Snowden, Isaac, 63
Snowden, Otto and Muriel, 120
Somerset Club, 66, 117
"Sons of Liberty," 31
South Boston, 34, 45, 48, 54, 62, 75, 87, 90, 95, 104, 108, 117, 120, 126, 132, 136, 139

Neighborhood & Street Index

DOWNTOWN BOSTON

Dock Square
340 Faneuil Hall Marketplace, 51
9 Marshall Street, 26
11 Marshall Street, 14
41 Union Street, 21, 51
45 Union Street, 40

Downtown
53 Boylston Street, 13
87 Boylston Street, 81
106 Boylston Street, 63, 95
20 Bromfield Street, 70
21 Bromfield Street, 63
21 Congress Street, 46
60 Congress Street, 54
Court Square, 5, 66, 67, 68
Court Street, 30
1 Court Street, 86
65 Court Street, 79
214 Devonshire Street, 44
Essex Street, 31
Exchange and State Streets, 40
5 Exeter Place, 80
1 Federal Street, 39, 46, 49, 71
Franklin Street, 124
Hamilton Place, 36, 67, 71, 72, 75, 84, 85
Hawley Street, 39
Milk Street, 17
17 Pearl Street, 54
3 School Street, 53, 70, 74
20 School Street, 38
27 School Street, 106
State Street, 31
State and Washington Streets, 10
27 State Street, 3, 4, 104
28 State Street, 24, 38
16 Summer Street, 25, 74
83–85 Summer Street, 78
Tremont Street, 11, 12, 32

10 Tremont Street, 39
17 Tremont Street, 51
58 Tremont Street, 29, 37, 48
82 Tremont Street, 56
88 Tremont Street, 58, 63, 65, 72
174 Tremont Street, 90
176 Tremont Street, 103
270 Tremont Street, 109
1 Washington Mall, 81, 134
Washington Street, 6, 17, 30, 126, 134
46 Washington Street, 56
121 Washington Street, 58
201 Washington Street, 16
210 Washington Street, 6
236–238 Washington Street, 6, 77
239 Washington Street, 4
268 Washington Street, 19
276–278 Washington Street, 88
301 Washington Street, 141
324 Washington Street, 53
327 Washington Street, 14
364 Washington Street, 85
417 Washington Street, 118
426 Washington Street, 101
539 Washington Street, 111
7 Water Street, 115
9 West Street, 50
15 West Street, 58
3 Winter Place, 89
24½ Winter Street, 71

Financial District
Broad Street, 57
Congress Street, 40
1 Federal Street, 46, 49, 71
160 Federal Street, 111
1 Lincoln Street, 145
3 McKinley Square, 62, 103
Purchase Street, 56
State Street, 68
53 State Street, 21, 25, 59

24 Eliot Street, 14
95 Forest Hills Avenue, 63
30 Germania Street, 136
10 Lamartine Street, 131
144 McBride Street, 49
South Street, 13
12 South Street, 30
125 The Arborway, 78
3484 Washington Street, 84

Kenmore
Commonwealth Avenue, 76
645 Beacon Street, 105

Mattapan
1257 Blue Hill Avenue, 139
1509 Blue Hill Avenue, 113
1060 Morton Street, 117

Mission Hill
125 Parker Hill Avenue, 89
St. Alphonsus Street, 138
1525 Tremont Street, 144

North End
Charter Street, 11
16 Charter Street, 70
600 Commercial Street, 120
Hanover Street, 21, 32, 66, 87
380 Hanover Street, 112
383 Hanover Street, 110
401 Hanover Street, 22
North Square, 9, 25
19 North Square, 14, 20
25 Parmenter Street, 56
98 Prince Street, 135
146 Prince Street, 72
193 Salem Street, 23, 29
11½ Thatcher Street, 109

North Station
Causeway Street, 67, 110
North Washington Street, 37

Roslindale
South Street and Archdale Road, 86

Roxbury
Blue Hill Avenue, 128
Blue Hill Avenue and Warren Street, 43
515 Blue Hill Avenue, 128
14 Crawford Street, 120
55 Dimock Street, 72
111 Dudley Street, 84
John Eliot Square, 3, 27
1 Malcolm X Boulevard, 145
16 Ronald Street, 127
One Schroeder Plaza, 68
59 Townsend Street, 96
1525 Tremont Street, 81, 144
1904 Washington Street, 130

South Boston
Broadway and H Street, 87
1663 Columbia Road, 75
70 Fargo Street, 62
95 G Street, 126
O Street, 117
308 West Broadway, 104

South End
Berkeley Street, 3
441 Columbus Avenue, 115
600 Columbus Avenue, 96
11 E. Newton Street, 75
133 E. Springfield Street, 73
444 Harrison Avenue, 125
761 Harrison Avenue, 74
8 Pine Street, 125
9 Rutland Square, 76
539 Tremont Street, 85, 99
791 Tremont Street, 67
20 Union Park, 88
40 Union Park Street, 114
Washington Street, 3
1400 Washington Street, 79

West End
Blossom Street, 91
Cambridge Street, 39
Causeway and Lowell Streets, 85
215 Charles Street, 5, 96
55 Fruit Street, 61

CPSIA information can be obtained at www.ICGtesting.com
Printed in the USA
LVOW12s2153111113

360944LV00020B/409/P

9 781933 212128